W9-BYV-264

BISHOP'S UNIVERSITY
LIBRARY
LENNOXVILLE

THE BRAZILIAN CAPITAL GOODS INDUSTRY

1929–1964

Written under the auspices of

The Center for International Affairs

and

The Center for Studies in Education and Development
Harvard University

THE BRAZILIAN CAPITAL GOODS INDUSTRY

1929–1964

———————————————————

NATHANIEL H. LEFF

HARVARD UNIVERSITY PRESS

Cambridge, Massachusetts 1968

© Copyright 1968 by the President and Fellows of Harvard College
All rights reserved
Distributed in Great Britain by Oxford University Press, London
Library of Congress Catalog Card Number 68-21976
Printed in the United States of America

To Judith,

Avraham, Chana, and Menachem

ACKNOWLEDGMENTS

I am glad for the opportunity to thank the many individuals and institutions who aided in the preparation of this study.

I have relied heavily on the data collected by the Fundação Getúlio Vargas of Rio de Janeiro, and I am grateful to Dr. Julian Chacel and Dr. Isaac Kerstenetzky for their collaboration. Information was also very kindly made available by Dr. Eduardo Gomes of SUMOC (Superintendência da Moeda e do Crédito); the São Paulo State Statistical Department; Petrobrás; and the São Paulo State Association of Equipment Manufacturers.

Dr. Aníbal Pinto of the ECLA-National Development Bank Study Group was kind enough to put an office at my disposal in Rio. The ABDIB (Associação Brasileira para o Desenvolvimento das Indústrias de Base) extended a similar service in São Paulo, and I am very grateful to Dr. Jorge de Rezende, Dr. Borelli, Dr. Bello, and Dona Marina da Nobruega of the Association, as well as to Dr. Einar Kok and the São Paulo State Association of Equipment Manufacturers, for their assistance in introducing me to their member firms. Paul Sturgis, Sebastão Advíncula da Cunha, Tarcísio Arantes, José Maria Villaça, Ary Bouzan, and Raimar Richers helped to get this study under way. I owe a very special debt to Dr. Nuno Fidelino de Figueiredo, Director of the ECLA Industrial Development Division, for sharing with me his extensive knowledge of Brazilian industry; and to Professor Antônio Delfim Netto of São Paulo University for discussion of macro-economic aspects of Brazilian development. Finally, I am very grateful to the many people in the firms studied and to the government and trade association officials who were kind enough to give extensively of their time for interviews. Since they were promised anonymity, I cannot thank them by name, but the material they were good enough to supply constitutes much of the basis for this study.

I am also most grateful to the Doherty Foundation and to the United States NDFL program for providing the specialized area

training and experience which enabled me to undertake the study;
to Professor Paul N. Rosenstein-Rodan for his help and for first
arousing my interest in Brazil; to Adam Curle of Harvard University's Center for Studies in Education and Development and
Edward S. Mason of the Harvard Center for International Affairs
for providing support and a stimulating place in which to work; to
Werner Baer, for an introduction to Brazil; to C. E. Beeby,
Samuel Bowles, Frank Bonilla, David Felix, Russell Davis,
Robinson Hollister, and Frank Levy for their comments on part of
the study. Some of this material was first presented in a series of
lectures at the United Nations' Instituto de Planificación
Económica y Social, at Santiago de Chile, where I benefited from
the comments of economists of several Latin American countries.

I owe a very special debt to R. S. Eckaus, Gordon Smith, and
Raymond Vernon for their careful reading and many valuable
suggestions on an earlier draft. Needless to say, I bear sole responsibility for any of the study's deficiencies. Robert Erwin helped
with his editing skills. I am also indebted to Nancy Brown, Peggy
Thompson, and Ann Bertram for their patience and care in
preparation of the manuscript.

Finally, I am grateful to Judith for her constant support and
encouragement.

November, 1967   Nathaniel H. Leff

CONTENTS

x   *Contents*

TABLES

THE BRAZILIAN CAPITAL GOODS INDUSTRY

1929–1964

ABBREVIATIONS

ABDIB	Associação Brasileira para o Desenvolvimento das Indústrias de Base (Brazilian Association for the Development of Basic Industry)
BNDE	Banco Nacional do Desenvolvimento Econômico (Brazilian National Development Bank)
ECE	United Nations Economic Commission for Europe
ECLA	United Nations Economic Commission for Latin America
EPEA	Escritório de Pesquisa Econômica Aplicada (Office for Applied Economic Research of the Brazilian Planning Ministry)
FGV	Fundação Getúlio Vargas (Getúlio Vargas Foundation)
GEIMAPE	Grupo Executivo para a Indústria Mecânica (Executive Group for the Mechanical Industry)
IBGE	Instituto Brasileira de Geografia e Estatística (Brazilian Institute of Geography and Statistics)
IBRD	International Bank for Reconstruction and Development
OECD	Organization for Economic Cooperation and Development
SENAI	Serviço Nacional de Aprendizagem Industrial (National Industrial Apprenticeship Service)
SUMOC	Superintendência da Moeda e do Crédito (Brazilian Monetary Authority)

I

INTRODUCTION

OUTLINE OF THE STUDY

This is a case study of industrial growth in Brazil, a country whose economy has been able to expand at a relatively high rate despite the well-known barriers of underdevelopment. Between 1947 and 1964, aggregate real output in Brazil grew approximately 152 percent, at an annual cumulative rate of 5.6 percent.[1] Industrial production led in this growth, increasing at a cumulative annual rate of 8.7 percent, as compared with 4.3 percent for agriculture. Table I-1 indicates the effects of this rapid industrial growth on the composition of Brazilian output.

Brazilian industrial growth in the postwar period has been based primarily on the development of new activities rather than the

TABLE I-1. Sectoral Distribution of Brazilian Domestic Product (Percent)

Sector	1947	1961
Agriculture	27	22
Industry	21	34
Others	52	44
	100	100

Source: Werner Baer, *Industrialization and Economic Development in Brazil* (Homewood, Ill., 1965), p. 71, Table 3-11. That table was computed from data in 1947 prices.

1. Real output in Brazil is estimated by the Fundação Getúlio Vargas of Rio de Janeiro (the semi-official research institution which compiles the Brazilian national income accounts). The series is a weighted average, using a moving base, of several sectoral indices for which physical data—e.g., on electricity generation—are available. For details, see Werner Baer, *Industrialization and Economic Development in Brazil* (Homewood, Ill., 1965), pp. 218–221. The Fundação states in its tables that real output is computed in constant (1949) prices.

expansion of traditional ones. In the period 1949–1959, growth was especially marked in the metallurgical, mechanical, electrical material, and transportation equipment industries. Whereas they had contributed approximately 15 percent of industrial value added in 1949, their participation had risen to 27 percent by 1959.[2] This near-doubling involved a structural change within the composition of industrial output and is all the more impressive because the industrial sector as a whole was also expanding so rapidly.

The analysis made here of Brazilian industrial development follows the approach of a disaggregated study. As a unit of study, an industry is both small enough for detailed analysis and large enough to permit some generalizations about the development process.[3] At the same time, an industry study can be useful for macro-economic analysis and planning; for in the absence of accurate disaggregated data, macro-models may be based upon a priori notions or casual empiricism. The industry under study is the capital goods industry. We will first discuss its history, to consider the genesis of this activity in an underdeveloped economy and its pattern of evolution. The next chapters are concerned with conditions of factor supply. In particular, how did the industry in its rapid growth overcome problems in the supply of capital, entrepreneurship, skilled workers, technically educated personnel, and "complex technology"? Available data did not permit a detailed examination of capital in the industry, but the general features of the picture are clear, and these are presented in the historical chapter.[4] We then consider the industry's demand conditions: the determinants of the size of the market for equipment

2. Data calculated from figures in IBGE (Instituto Brasileiro de Geografia e Estatística), *Censo Industrial* (Rio de Janeiro, 1963).

3. Cf. the discussion by W. W. Rostow, "Some General Reflections," in National Bureau of Economic Research, *Capital Formation and Economic Growth* (Princeton, N.J., 1955), pp. 647–648.

4. Not all firms publish balance sheets, and those that do are not subject to supervision of the sort that insures a measure of full disclosure and uniformity in concepts. Furthermore, the usefulness of the published data on capital size and structure is greatly reduced by the accounting practices followed during the Brazilian inflation. In the course of the inflation, real replacement values for fixed capital assets have diverged increasingly from historical book values. However, firms have not followed consistent practices in the revaluation of their fixed capital assets. Many balance sheets report these assets at historical value, which is now only a fraction of replacement value in current cruzeiros. Consequently, values for fixed assets often give a seriously distorted picture both of real capital values and of the structure of assets. By the same token, elaborations of these data which do not take cognizance of the distortions—e.g., articles in *Conjuntura Econômica* and *Editorial Banas*—are also misleading.

in Brazil; the domestic industry's ability to compete with imports in carving out a share of this total market; and the market structure within which firms have competed. Finally, we discuss the economic effects of the industry's growth and its place in future Brazilian economic development.[5]

At times, our discussion of conditions in this industry has implications for broader questions of Brazilian industrial development. The capital goods industry (and especially the subsector focused upon for this part of the analysis) has high demands both for technically educated manpower and for specialized skilled labor. Because low and inelastic supply of these inputs is sometimes considered a serious barrier to economic development, this sector constitutes an interesting case study of a resolution of the problem. The industry's experience in the absorption of advanced technology also offers an opportunity for a study in depth. Discussion of these issues benefits from being placed within a concrete economic context, with other conditions specified, rather than being treated in the abstract.

Analysis of demand conditions in the capital goods industry leads to a discussion of savings and investment in the course of the Brazilian development process. The industry's experience in competing with imports and enlarging its share of the domestic market is an interesting case in import substitution. Development of the capital goods industry may also have important implications for Brazilian macro-economic growth; as a major source of investment goods, its demand and supply conditions affect the overall rate of capital formation. This question is especially interesting in Brazil. As in some other less-developed countries, the conventional view is that capital formation has been constrained by insufficient capital goods supply, because of dependence on income-inelastic supply of imports for most investment goods. As Celso Furtado puts it: "It is a general characteristic of underdeveloped economies that their capital formation processes depend greatly on foreign trade. This dependency occurs not only in connection with the formation of savings, but mainly in regard to the transformation of savings into real investments . . . As the economic structure passes into the intermediate and higher stages of underdevelopment . . .

5. The outline followed draws heavily on Everett Hagen's *Handbook for Industry Studies* (Glencoe, Ill., 1958), with some adaptations for the special issues raised by this particular industry.

while the formation of saving becomes less dependent on the export
sector, it is almost always accompanied . . . by greater dependency
in the transformation of savings into real capital."[6]

This interpretation also attributes a major role to dependence on
imported capital goods in generating inflation and balance-of-
payments problems.[7] By the same token, development of a domestic
capital goods industry is claimed to overcome these problems and
permit accelerated rates of growth.[8] These issues are also related to
the imperialism question, for growth of domestic capital goods
supply is expected to permit both more economic independence and
greater autonomy from foreign political and cultural manipulation.

Finally, the capital goods industry is of special policy interest in
Brazil because of the prominent place it is often accorded as a
"leading sector" for future economic growth.[9] In this view, growth
of the economy in the 1950's was stimulated by import substitution
of consumer durables, but development in "the next phase" will
depend on accelerated domestic production of capital goods. Our
analysis should shed some light on the extent to which demand and
supply conditions make it feasible to speak of this central role for
the capital goods industry.

RESEARCH METHODOLOGY

For the purpose of this study, the capital goods industry was
defined as the manufacturers of producers' equipment. In the
Brazilian industrial census classification, this includes sections of the
metallurgical, mechanical, electrical material, and transportation
equipment industries. Passenger automobiles and consumer
durables have been excluded.

6. Celso Furtado, *Development and Underdevelopment*, trans. R. W. de Aguiar and E. C.
Drysdale (Berkeley, 1964), pp. 150–151.
7. *Ibid.*, p. 154: "These examples suggest that for a given rate of increase in world trade
the rate of growth compatible with internal [monetary] stability . . . is far higher in developed
than in underdeveloped structures. This circumstance explains, on the one hand, the slower
growth of underdeveloped economies during the past few decades, and accounts, on the other,
for the well known tendency to disequilibrium in the balance of payments observed in all
underdeveloped countries which endeavor in one way or another to intensify their rate of
growth."
8. E.g., Celso Furtado in *Desenvolvimento e Subdesenvolvimento*, 2 ed. (Rio de Janeiro, 1963),
pp. 206–210, 242, 259.
9. See, e.g., "Auge y Declinación del Proceso de Sustitución de Importaciones in el
Brasil," *Boletín Económico de América Latina*, 9 (March 1964), 59–62.

The statistical material that is the basis for the study comes largely from the Brazilian national income accounts' time-series on income and investment, from the industrial censuses, from a 1960 survey conducted by the São Paulo Association of Equipment Producers, and from several specialized ECLA (United Nations Economic Commission for Latin America) studies. These materials permitted an analysis of the industry's demand conditions, competition with imports, and its effects on Brazilian economic development. Available resources, however, did not permit a detailed study of the entire Brazilian capital goods industry's history, conditions of manpower supply and utilization, absorption of complex technology, and market structure.[10] Consequently, with respect to these questions the discussion focuses mainly on one sector, heavy-engineering products. This is the group of firms producing equipment for the electrical, metallurgical, chemical, petroleum, paper, and cement industries.[11] Information from well-informed observers in the equipment industry's trade associations, however, and scattered interviewing of machinery producers in other subsectors indicate that the origins and historical evolution of the heavy-engineering products sector are similar to those of the industry as a whole. The material on manpower and on advanced technology is also broadly applicable, though demands on the latter by the heavy-engineering sector are the strongest in the entire industry. The situation as regards market structure varies with individual products. Hence, except when otherwise stated, the picture presented in these chapters also applies to the broader capital goods industry.[12]

The heavy-engineering products sector offered several special advantages for study. Although the number of firms (20) was small enough to permit direct inquiry by a single researcher, their share in aggregate Brazilian equipment production is relatively large,

---

10. The 1960 Brazilian industrial census lists 25,551 firms manufacturing producers' goods. Hence, it was beyond the capacity of a single researcher, even working with a stratified sample, to cover all of them satisfactorily.

11. The products manufactured by firms of the sector fall under the following classifications in the *Standard Industrial Classification Manual*: 3443, 3444, 3511, 3535, 3536, 3551, 3554, 3559, 3567.

12. Throughout the study, for the sake of clarity, "the industry" will refer to the equipment industry as a whole, while "the sector" refers to the heavy-engineering products sector within the industry.

exceeded only by automotive equipment.[13] Because of the prominence of the sector's several client industries in the Brazilian output mix, and because of their high capital/output ratios, they are expected to account for a large share of future Brazilian equipment purchases.[14] Furthermore, as shown below, the heavy-engineering products sector poses in especially acute form some problems of specialized manpower demands. Finally, other aspects of the sector had been studied by the Industrial Development Division of ECLA, so that some material was already available.[15]

Field work for the study was undertaken in Brazil between November 1963 and December 1964. Nine months were spent in São Paulo, where most of the companies and their clients and suppliers are located. Four months were spent in Rio de Janeiro for interviews with the remaining firms, and with the government planning agencies and the import and monetary authorities that have affected the industry's development.

The trade association, to which most of the sector's firms belong, facilitated introductions to its members. Good access was also possible to the companies that do not belong to the association. Because the characteristics of the population were not known before the study, sampling methods could not be used, and interviews were conducted in all of the 20 firms that compose the sector. The inquiry relied heavily on direct interviewing, though, when possible, written questionnaires were also filled out by the firms. Interviewing technique consisted of the formulation of open-ended questions which permitted interviewees to respond freely and at length about the subjects raised. Data brought out in the first interviews served

13. Another possible contender is the Brazilian machine-tool industry. Data in the ECLA study of that industry, however, indicate that the value of machine-tool production has been less than half of heavy-engineering products. See *Las Máquinas-Herramientas en el Brasil* (*La Fabricación de Maquinarias y Equipos Industriales en América Latina*, vol. 2 [New York: United Nations, 1962]), pp. 25, 45.

14. The IBRD mission to Brazil, in "Manufacturing Industry" ("Current Economic Position and Prospects of Brazil," vol. 5, mimeographed [1965]), p. 10 and Annex B, estimated that the sector's client industries would take more than one third of all fixed investment in Brazilian manufacturing in the 1960's. As noted in Chap. V, manufacturing has taken approximately 25% of all equipment in Brazil, so that this means approximately 8% of aggregate equipment demand. The electricity industry, another of the sector's clients, has taken approximately 11% of all Brazilian equipment purchases. Hence the sector's clients are expected to account for almost 20% of total equipment purchases.

15. The ECLA study referred to is *Basic Equipment in Brazil* (*The Manufacture of Industrial Machinery and Equipment in Latin America*, vol. 1 [New York: United Nations, 1963]). It deals primarily with projections of the demand of the client industries cited over the period 1961–1970, and of the capacity of Brazilian equipment manufacturers to supply it.

as the basis for questions in subsequent sessions until the topic was exhausted. Interviews were usually held with several officials in each firm. In addition to the general managers, the officials in charge of production, sales, personnel, and finance were questioned. In the course of factory visits, foremen and bench workers were also interviewed. Interviewees were generally cooperative, and sometimes as many as fifteen hours were spent in the course of five or more visits to individual firms.

To complete the analysis, interviews were conducted in the several metallurgical companies which are the sector's principal suppliers, and in many of the firms that are its clients. On matters of finance, officials of local banks and finance companies were consulted. In order to gain some perspective on the sector, several companies producing automotive equipment, machine tools, and diesel engines were questioned. In all, intensive interviews were carried out in 44 companies. Finally, for a check on the research, the author spoke with some of the international consultant firms that have an intimate knowledge of this sector, both in Brazil and other countries. Throughout this study, data from a source not otherwise cited derive from interview material.

II

ORIGINS AND EVOLUTION OF THE

HEAVY-ENGINEERING PRODUCTS SECTOR

Contrary to some impressions, the Brazilian capital goods industry is not a recent development, the "final stage" of an industrialization that began with finished products and proceeded by backward linkages to producers' goods. Equipment production developed relatively early in Brazil's industrial history, and by 1947–1949 domestic industry supplied approximately 61 percent of all producers' equipment in Brazil.[1] This domestic supply coefficient was more than three times larger than in Argentina during the same years.[2] Moreover, the Brazilian industry was no artificial creation fostered by government protection. On the contrary, until the early 1960's it had to meet the competition of equipment imports which were accorded preferential exchange-rate treatment and duty-free importation.

The heavy-engineering products sector has developed to the point where an ECLA study estimates it as capable of supplying approximately 80 percent of the equipment demanded by the Brazilian electricity, petroleum, petrochemical, paper, metallurgical, and cement industries.[3] In this development, Brazil is relatively unique, for it is one of the few underdeveloped countries to have achieved such a supply capability.

1. Calculated from data kindly supplied by the Fundação Getúlio Vargas. An ECLA study of import substitution in Brazil, "Auge y Declinación del Proceso de Sustitución de Importaciones in el Brasil," *Boletín Económico de América Latina*, 9 (March 1964), 16, Table 5, shows even higher participation by domestic industry in aggregate equipment supply for those years—79%.

2. Calculated from data in Carlos Diaz-Alejandro, "Relative Prices and Capital Formation in the Argentine Republic," mimeographed (New Haven: Yale University Economic Growth Center, 1965), Tables 1 and 8.

3. *Basic Equipment in Brazil* (*The Manufacture of Industrial Machinery and Equipment in Latin America*, vol. 1 [New York: United Nations, 1963]), pp. 4–5.

ORIGINS

THE SECTOR'S BEGINNINGS, 1880–1929

Before discussing the sector's history, which dates mainly from the 1930's, let us briefly consider its economic seedbed. Specifically, where in an export economy did the beginnings of equipment manufacture emerge? On the supply side, where did such capabilities as the necessary production equipment, specialized labor skills, and technical ability and innovating entrepreneurship in management develop? Furthermore, what were the sources of demand for equipment in an underdeveloped economy, and how could local producers compete with imports in a period without tariff protection and with ample foreign exchange?

During Brazil's heyday as an export economy, demand for mechanical products came from several sources. Transportation equipment was the equipment product in greatest demand for local use. Despite relative factor prices different from those in the advanced countries, railways—and later automobiles and trucks—replaced traditional means of conveyance. Export agriculture provided another important client. Equipment for the processing of coffee, sugar, and cotton was among the first mechanical products introduced into the Brazilian economy. For processing these products, in contrast to their production, it was found advantageous to use modern equipment.[4] Military technology was also an important source of demand; the Brazilian army and navy were early users of mechanical products. Finally, some equipment was used in the construction industry, especially in building infrastructure facilities for the economy's foreign trade.

Largely because of locational advantages, part of this demand could be met economically by local producers. For storage tanks and for the bulky, inexpensive boilers that went into much processing equipment, the ratio of transport cost to the FOB value of imports was so high that local producers had a competitive advantage. Local workshops could also compete effectively for repair work. Foundry work, both for final products and for maintenance,

4. Warren Dean, in his "São Paulo's Industrial Elite, 1890–1960" (Ph.D. diss., University of Florida, 1964), pp. 62–65, tells the story of one firm which in the 1880's began production of a coffee-hulling machine, on the basis of design's made by a second-generation German immigrant, and subsequently expanded into manufacture of other agricultural equipment, railway coaches, and various metal structures.

TABLE II-1. Share of the Metallurgical and Equipment Industries in Total Value Added of Brazilian Manufacturing, 1920, 1940, 1950 (Percent)

Industry	1920	1940	1950
Metallurgical	4.3	7.7	7.4
Equipment	2.0	5.8	6.2
	6.3	13.5	13.6

Source: Calculated from Werner Baer, *Industrialization and Economic Development in Brazil* (Homewood, Ill., 1965), p. 17, Table 2-1.

was another area where local suppliers were able to compete with imports. In particular, the equipment importers often did not maintain adequate stocks of spare parts, and it was sometimes more economical to cast a part locally than to wait for importation. As a result, local foundries and repair shops for automotive and railway equipment were a particularly important seedbed for the development of domestic supply capacity. The maintenance divisions for the processing equipment of the large coffee, sugar, and cotton plantations also developed into small-scale mechanical workshops. For reasons of national security, the army and especially the navy maintained some capacity for repair of their equipment. In the early days, some of the best equipment and personnel were found in the military arsenals.

These early activities of Brazilian equipment manufacture were important both for their immediate contribution to output and for the basis they provided for subsequent development. In 1907, an industrial census of the Rio de Janeiro area showed that approximately 18 percent of all industrial workers were in foundries and metalworking firms.[5] In 1920 the industrial census for the whole country showed that even after the rapid growth of the textile and food industries during the first decades of the century, approximately 8 percent of the industrial work-force was in the machinery industry.[6] These activities also provided the seedbed where even in

5. Calculated from data in George Wythe, "Brazil: Trends in Industrial Development," in *Economic Growth: Brazil, India, Japan*, ed. S. S. Kuznets et al. (Durham, N.C., 1955), p. 39.

6. Dean ("São Paulo's Industrial Elite," p. 72) presents rough data which show an annual cumulative growth rate of 9.5% in São Paulo industrial production between 1905 and 1915. His material shows the preponderance of the textile and food-processing industries in this growth. The percentage of work-force in the machinery industry was calculated from data on the 1920 census, presented in Werner Baer, *Industrialization and Economic Development in Brazil* (Homewood, Ill., 1965), p. 251.

an export economy with unobstructed importation some domestic supply capabilities in the mechanical industries could develop. Once local firms had accumulated sufficient capital and "know-how" to produce full-fledged equipment installations, which, for reasons discussed below, yielded higher returns, they entered that field and left much of their previous light foundry and repair work to other firms that lacked the entrepreneurial and technical capacity to make this transition.

THE CAPITAL GOODS INDUSTRY, 1929–1945

Table II–1 presents data on the share of the equipment and the metallurgical industries—the latter included because of its large share of fabricated products such as castings and forgings—in total value added of Brazilian manufacturing during the industrial census years 1920 and 1940. For the sake of historical perspective on subsequent developments, 1950 is also included. These industries already had a significant portion of value added in Brazilian manufacturing as early as 1920. By 1940, however, they had grown rapidly enough to double their share. The equipment industry grew

TABLE II-2. Iron and Steel Consumption in Brazil, 1929–1940

Year	Index	Percentage change over preceding year
1929	100	14
1930	57	−43
1931	36	−37
1932	39	9
1933	70	91
1934	83	18
1935	103	24
1936	116	12
1937	152	31
1938	142	−6
1939	166	17
1940	186	12

Source: Calculated from statistics in Werner Baer, *Industrialization and Economic Development in Brazil,* (Homewood, Ill., 1965), p. 23, Table 2-4.

at a particularly disproportionate rate, almost tripling its percentage. This growth is especially impressive since other industries, particularly textiles, were also expanding rapidly through the middle and late 1930's.[7] Rather than being a late development, these industries by 1940 had attained the fairly important position within the structure of Brazilian manufacturing that they had ten years later, in 1950.

The growth of equipment production seems to have been especially rapid in the period 1933–1940. Output statistics are not available for those years, but Table II–2 shows data on Brazilian consumption of iron and steel. Because this was before the extensive use of iron and steel either in high-rise construction or in a consumer durables industry, these input figures give an indication of Brazilian equipment production. As we see, demand for metallurgical products began to recover in 1932, reached its 1929 levels by 1935, and continued with substantial annual increases through most of the late 1930's.[8] The annual compound rate of growth between 1933 and 1940 was 10.1 percent.

TABLE II-3. Production of Equipment in Brazil, 1939–1947

Year	Index	Percentage change over preceding year
1939	100	—
1940	108	8
1941	96	−11
1942	78	−19
1943	84	8
1944	133	57
1945	117	−12
1946	170	45
1947	236	39

Source: Calculated from CEPAL-BNDE, *Análise e Projeções do Desenvolvimento Econômico* (Rio de Janeiro, 1956), p. 88, Table XXIII.

7. Baer, *Economic Development in Brazil*, pp. 24–26, and Celso Furtado, *A Formação Econômica do Brasil*, 5 ed. (Rio de Janeiro, 1963), pp. 228–231.
8. The year 1932 was also the turning point for other Brazilian industries during the depression. They subsequently expanded output rapidly throughout the 1930's. Cf. Baer, *Economic Development in Brazil*, p. 21, Table 2-3.

In the early years of World War II, however, equipment production declined, and in 1945 it stood only 9 percent higher than in 1940. In Table II–3, we see data on annual percentage change in Brazilian equipment production during World War II and the early postwar years. The decline in output in the early war years is noteworthy, the more so because it occurred during a period when national income and demand were rising rapidly. These data, moreover, contradict the conventional idea that by curtailing supply from traditional overseas sources, World War II had a sharp stimulating effect on Brazilian industrialization.[9] They also run counter to the view that the equipment industries were a creation of the war.

In discussing the impact of the limitations in normal overseas supply, however, we should distinguish between a "demand-diverting" effect and a "supply-constraint" effect. That is, one effect of import stringency was to divert demand from traditional suppliers to domestic producers. At the same time, however, lack of raw materials and other inputs from overseas constrained the domestic supply response to this additional demand. The domestic industries that did grow rapidly during the war were those, notably textiles, which benefited from the demand diversion, but which also had elastic supply of their inputs from local sources. In industries like equipment, however, although the demand-diverting effect was present and offered favourable market conditions, the supply constraint imposed by insufficient availability of steel from both domestic and overseas sources prevented output from increasing rapidly.

This explanation of the relatively limited wartime expansion of capital goods production, particularly during the early war years, is lent some support by Table II–4. To highlight the relation of input supply and equipment production, the previous statistics on output of equipment are presented alongside figures of steel supply. This fluctuated throughout those years in response to foreign supply allocations, availability of shipping, and the German blockade.

9. See, for example, Baer's indiscriminate statement (*Industrial Development in Brazil*, p. 44): "The war was a powerful stimulant to the further industrialization of Brazil due to the drastic curtailment of imports." This was true for certain industries, but other industries had their expansion curtailed for lack of imported inputs. The aggregate growth rate for Brazilian manufacturing was lower during the war years than in the postwar period. (See the data in Table 8, p. 15, of Grupo Misto BNDE-CEPAL, *Análise e Projeções do Desensolvimento Econômico* [Rio de Janeiro, 1957]).

TABLE II-4. Domestic Equipment Output and Aggregate Steel Supply, 1940–1947 (Percentage Changes)

Year	Output of equipment products	Steel supply
1940	8	−2
1941	−11	−8
1942	−19	−28
1943	8	20
1944	57	46
1945	−12	−5
1946	45	48
1947	39	13

Sources: Data on equipment production are from Table II-3 above. Data on annual steel supply are from América Barbosa de Oliveira, "Mercado Presente e Futuro do Aço," *Boletim da Associação Brasileira de Metais*, 19 (January 1963), Appendix Table 1.

Equipment production and steel supply were closely related in both the direction and magnitude of their annual percentage changes. Because demand conditions were consistently favorable on account of the wartime boom, the direction of causality probably runs from availability of raw materials to increased output of equipment.

This hypothesis concerning the importance of supply constraints is also supported by the behavior of the capital goods industry in the early postwar years. Although equipment imports were generally available without restrictions, the domestic industry's output expanded much more rapidly than during the war, when it had been freer of competitive import pressures. This suggests that removal of the supply constraint through increased availability of inputs from abroad more than compensated for the end of the demand-diverting effect from import restriction.

The data on the growth of the capital goods industry during the 1930's, and particularly its share as early as 1940 in the structure of Brazilian manufacturing output, indicate the early development of domestic equipment supply. In Chapter VIII we will discuss the extent to which this balanced growth in capital goods production may have facilitated Brazilian growth under subsequent conditions of inelastic import supply. We have also noted the constraint on the industry's output imposed by inadequate raw material supply during the war. These difficulties were subsequently corrected with the resumption of overseas supply for many inputs, and with large-scale domestic steel production from the newly established Volta Redonda steel mill.

DOMESTIC FIRMS, 1930–1945

Let us now consider the origins of the heavy-engineering sector's domestic firms, beginning with market conditions and then proceeding to questions of factor supply.

There are several reasons for the sector's market viability during this period when, as has been mentioned earlier, imports were permitted without tariffs, import quotas, or other forms of protection. First, as mentioned above, for some activities domestic firms had the advantage of localization factors. Production of custom-made equipment installations is also relatively labor-intensive, because wage costs are approximately 60 percent of value added in production.[10] Moreover, Brazilian firms concentrated on the lighter engineering products, in which the incidence of labor costs is especially high.[11] Hence they had the advantage of producing a labor-intensive product in a low-wage economy. Furthermore, according to the sector's company managers, economies of scale are not very important in the manufacture of these custom-made products. Consequently, the sector avoided the situation of comparatively high costs dictated by a relatively small domestic market and by technology with rapidly declining marginal costs.[12]

Finally, local producers could often compete favorably with imports because of the credit which they extended to clients. In Brazil, would-be purchasers of capital goods have rarely been able to obtain long-term bank finance. In addition, smaller and less-

10. The points in this paragraph are also made in the ECLA report, *Basic Equipment in Brazil*, pp. 59–60. According to the sector's foreign company managers, production of heavy-equipment installations in the advanced countries uses a similar technology, and is also highly labor-intensive.

11. Data provided by firms of the sector.

12. While the high labor-intensity and the absence of significant economies of scale in production of custom-made equipment were certainly important in this sector's ability to compete with imports, these special features should not be exaggerated. In Chap. VI we see that the broader Brazilian capital goods industry producing series-made equipment, in which these particular advantages did not apply, was also able to meet the price competition of imports.

known client firms have not had access to foreign credits to finance equipment imports. Therefore, local producers were able to maintain themselves by acting as bankers to such clients and supplying the credit for equipment purchases. This financing, amounting perhaps to 30 percent of the purchase price over a one-year period, was often crucial for maintaining sales and output of some domestic firms.

The sector's initial demands for factors were resolved when market conditions were favourable enough to permit derived demands attracting capital and skilled labor from elsewhere in the economy. Subsequent development was facilitated as production in earlier periods generated an increased supply of inputs—for example, capital from profit reinvestment and skilled manpower from learning in the course of production—which, again under favorable market conditions, could be retained in the sector for further expansion.

The domestic firms drew their original capital in about equal proportions from three sources in the economy. The firms that began as small mechanical workshops or foundries had relatively low capital requirements. With buoyant demand and profits, as well as high reinvestment rates since the middle 1930's, they have achieved their present capacity. The export and import trades were another source of capital. In this case, capital was attracted by the prospect of high profits from pioneering in products whose demand was expected to grow rapidly in the course of Brazilian economic development. Client industries have been a final source of capital, as large metallurgical firms expanded their maintenance departments into full-fledged plants manufacturing equipment. The parent companies followed this course because of their belief that by producing their own equipment they lower the cost of their capital formation. Based on these original sources of capital, firms have expanded by plowing back their profits. Profit reinvestment rates on the order of 75 percent maintained over the years have given the sector's domestic firms their present capacity.

The sector's entrepreneurs derive from two sources. First, entrepreneurship came from immigrants, usually of Italian origin, who arrived in Brazil at the turn of the last century. Working on the railroads or in one of the São Paulo mechanical workshops, they learned the trade of master mechanics and accumulated the savings to open their own workshops. Brilliant mechanics, they built their firms to the size of fifty or more employees before leadership passed to the hands of the second generation, in the 1930's and 1940's. The entrepreneurial capacity and technical abilities of the founders' sons was of crucial importance, for upon them depended the successful transition from workshop to factory. In family firms that were able to make this leap, the second generation almost always attended engineering school, in São Paulo or abroad.

Entrepreneurship also came from native-born Brazilians, often descendants of the traditional coffee elite, who attended engineering school in São Paulo during the 1920's and 1930's. Aside from their technical instruction, these engineers imbibed an "industrial mentality" and a nationalistic ideology which apparently had its origins in the São Paulo Polytechnical School, an institution founded by nationalist modernizers and Comtian positivists in the 1890's.[13] People in the sector refer consciously to this "industrial mentality" in contrast to the "commercial mentality" that they believe prevails elsewhere in Brazil. Because these ideas were important in orienting the sons of the native elite and of the immigrants and attracting them to the industry, they are worth considering in some detail.

The "industrial mentality" stressed the glamorous achievements of modern technology. Along with this attitude, sometimes bordering on scientism, the ideology emphasized a willingness to engage in the day-to-day details of technical work in order to participate in the world of modern technology and to help establish it in Brazil. Moreover, because the proponents of this ideology were most aware of the achievements of modern technology in industry rather than in agriculture, they were enthusiastic advocates of industrialization for Brazil. Strongly nationalistic, they also stressed the importance of import substitution as a means toward national economic and political progress.[14]

The formation of this mentality was most marked in the Institute for Technological Research at the São Paulo Polytechnical

13. See Ivan Lins, *História do Positivismo no Brasil* (São Paulo, 1964), pp. 140–141.

14. The ideology clearly incorporated some of the ideas of straightforward protectionism of the Friedrich List type, but the emphasis was always on the value of modern science and technology rather than the economic gains from industrialization. Hence the group that campaigned for these ideas devoted their efforts to founding a polytechnical school rather than lobbying for tariff protection.

School.[15] Most of the better engineering students worked at the Institute, where these views on modern technology and Brazilian development had been well elaborated by the 1920's. Some of the ideas are clearly stated in a speech by Dr. Paula Souza, the School's founder and dominant influence,[16] at the Polytechnical School's inauguration in 1894: "Yes, Gentlemen, if technical knowledge were taught to our people, we would have ... a diversified, prosperous, and well-managed industry ... In our own land we would easily have what we must now import with great expense from foreigners."[17]

This ideology also expressed a strong preference for industries that were considered the embodiment of both national development and modern technology. For example, steel, petroleum, and capital goods production had a special mystique and were accorded a higher value than textiles or food products.

The economic results of these attitudes made themselves felt as the graduates of the engineering schools showed a pioneering willingness to establish the enterprises that were to become the Brazilian capital goods industry. Because of this ideology, "glamorous" industries such as capital goods were able to attract entrepreneurial resources relatively easily. For example, some entrepreneurs explain their early move with their capital from textiles to the metallurgical and mechanical industries in terms of the greater enthusiasm which the latter evoked. The promise of high profits was certainly also present; but the "idealist" and "romantic" feelings toward modern technology and capital production—as the sector's entrepreneurs themselves describe their early attitudes—were crucial in ensuring that when objective economic conditions for the sector's development appeared, the opportunity would not go wasted.[18]

---

15. Although the ideology included many of the same attitudes as Brazilian nationalist ideology, students and professors of the Polytechnical School were enthusiastic supporters of the 1932 regionalist rebellion against Getúlio Vargas; and they took an active part in weapons design and manufacture to equip the São Paulo forces in the face of the arms blockade.

16. Dr. Souza is an interesting figure in the history of Brazilian nationalism and modernization. Son of a coffee planter, he studied engineering in Europe, fought in Garibaldi's army, returned to a successful career in São Paulo politics at the time of the Independence movement, and then began his lifework, the creation of the São Paulo Polytechnical Institute.

17. Quoted in J. L. Meiller and F. I. de Araújo Silva, *Meio Século de Tecnologia* (São Paulo, 1949), p. 28.

18. Brazilian economic history shows numerous cases of entrepreneurs who pioneered in

Requirements for administrative and technical manpower have generally been met by the local engineering schools. As discussed in Chapter III, rapid Brazilian industrialization and sharply growing demands for technical personnel have been accompanied by sustained increases in the supply of engineers. The sector's first requirements for highly trained shop personnel were filled largely from the seedbed areas mentioned earlier. Immigrants who had come to Brazil from countries with more advanced industrial development were another early source of skills and production experience.

Finally, the sector's domestic firms were also able to acquire sufficient "know-how" and technical capacity to produce engineering products. Machinery imports were the major channel for the early transmission of technology. The firms that started as repair shops or maintenance departments had years of long and intimate experience with imported machines, and on the basis of this they built their own products. Modifications were sometimes introduced to take account of differences in local raw materials or the smaller scale of production of some clients, but the equipment was modeled largely on the products developed in the advanced countries.

Technical literature from the developed countries was another very important, if undramatic, means by which firms acquired their technological capacity. In this case, the educational level of the Brazilian managers enabled them to learn a great deal from specifications in brochures and catalogs. Immigrant technicians and engineers were another valuable source of know-how for some firms. Often only one engineer with production experience from an advanced country provided sufficient knowledge to permit expansion into new processes and products.

In addition, the Technological Research Institute of the São Paulo Polytechnic School played an important role in promoting the early technical development of this and other São Paulo industries. Especially during the 1930's and 1940's, the Institute functioned as a central laboratory for all São Paulo industry. In order to carry on these efforts, the Institute was of a respectable size. In 1949, it employed a staff of 62 engineers and scientists, as

new economic activities that failed for lack of favorable objective conditions. Examples range from the Barão de Mauá's shipbuilding ventures in the nineteenth century to an effort at initiating airplane production in Piracicaba in the 1930's.

well as complementary technicians and administrative personnel.[19] The Institute did most of the materials testing required for the use of local raw materials. It also functioned as a technological pioneer, introducing previously unknown practices and processes from abroad. In both cases, the Institute overcame the problem of the large minimum scale for research and development efforts that prevented most local firms from maintaining their own laboratories during this period. In the 1950's, as firms entered new and more complex product lines, these channels for the transmission of complex technology were complemented by licensing agreements with firms in the advanced countries.

EVOLUTION OF THE SECTOR: POSTWAR TO 1960

After the end of World War II, output in the sector as well as in the entire capital goods industry grew very rapidly. In the capital goods industry as a whole, between the industrial census years of 1949 and 1959, beginning from a base of approximately 5.7 billion (1949) cruzeiros (about 306 million dollars), value added increased some 166 percent in real terms.[20] This amounted to an annual cumulative growth rate of 10.3 percent over the ten-year period. In heavy-engineering products, annual output expanded from approximately 30 million dollars after World War II to approximately 210 million dollars, of which some 140 million dollars was value added, in 1964.[21] This growth came both from expansion of the existing domestic firms and from output of the foreign firms that began production in Brazil during this period.

In achieving this growth, the sector's domestic firms made some important internal changes. To finance expansion, most firms had

19. Meiller and Silva, *Meio Século de Tecnologia*, p. 141.

20. Calculated from 1949 and 1959 figures in IBGE, *Censo Industrial* (Rio de Janeiro, 1963). In the case of "Automotive equipment," 80% of value added was considered "capital goods." This is in accordance with information supplied by GEIA (Grupo Executivo da Indústria Automobilística) concerning the percentage of truck and bus production in output of the automotive industries. The price deflator used in index 63, Metallurgical Products, published in *Conjuntura Econômica*. The exchange-rate used for this and subsequent dollar calculations is the average import rate for the year. These data were kindly made available by the Research Division of SUMOC.

21. The figure for 1964 is from p. 46 of the ECLA study, "Brasil: La Exportación de Manufacturas, sus Antecedentes y sus Posibilidades" (mimeographed, Santiago, Chile, 1966). The figure for the early postwar period is a rough approximation, calculated from data supplied by firms of the sector.

recourse to equity capital from outside of their original family groups.[22] Although the families still retained majority position and control, outside capital was accepted. This came through joint ventures with foreign firms, from the Brazilian development bank, or via the Brazilian stock exchange, from sales to the general public and mutual funds. This capital was used for expanded facilities and particularly for the larger equipment needed in production of "heavier" product lines. As they began to manufacture new and more complex products, all companies also concluded foreign licensing agreements of various sorts. In addition, firms expanded their own technical capacity by substantially increasing the number of engineering and technical personnel they employed.

THE PATTERN OF EVOLUTION

The sector's growth in the 1950's came largely from entry into new and broader product markets rather than from expansion within the same products of its older line. One common course was through entry into products that were "heavier," more "technically complex," and higher-quality versions of previous lines. According to the firms, "heavier" in this sense usually meant products whose manufacture required greater unit capital-intensity. "More complex" products required inputs of technical knowledge and production experience previously lacking in the economy. For example, most boilermakers in the sector began making light storage tanks and expanded by producing boilers for higher temperatures and pressures. By the early 1960's, they were producing boilers which operated at pressures up to 450 pounds per square inch. Similarly, producers of electrical transformers began with small (100 kVA) units, and expanded by producing heavier and more technically sophisticated units, reaching 20,000 kVA.

Firms also entered new markets by forward or backward integration, producing goods they formerly bought from suppliers or making final products for which they previously supplied components. For example, a producer of overhead cranes who had

22. The only domestic companies which did not bring in outside capital were those that were connected with companies in the metallurgical industry and could call upon their resources, or those that (in contrast with the more common pattern of expansion into several different product markets discussed below) maintained very strong market positions by specializing in a single product line.

bought his electrical motors from outside suppliers began to produce these motors, first for his own needs and then for other clients. In another case, an equipment producer integrated backward into the metallurgical industry. Investing in a blast furnace, rolling mill, and foundry, he supplied steel both for himself and for the broader market.

Finally, firms often chose new product lines on the basis of the public sector's investment program by installing capacity to supply equipment for the industries promoted by government policy. Public investments became especially important after 1956, when energetic efforts were taken to increase domestic output of many "basic products" such as steel and refined petroleum. As the government began to develop these industries and offered the prospect of favorable new markets, several firms in the heavy-engineering sector installed capacity to supply them. In one important case, that of equipment for the public sector petroleum company, firms entered the market after direct negotiations with the government corporation concerning its future equipment demands.

The sector followed this pattern of expansion into new and broader product lines for several reasons. Many smaller firms had entered the market for simpler products, such as light boiler work, and their competition depressed profit margins in the traditional products. By contrast, competitive pressures were less intense in the heavier and more complex products. Here, minimum-scale conditions limited access of the smaller companies to domestic and foreign credits for purchases of heavier fabricating equipment.[23]

23. The movement to heavier product lines has been an irreversible process in the sense that once firms made the transition, they could no longer compete effectively with the smaller firms in the lighter products. This became very important with the development of excess capacity in the more complex products in the early 1960's, as the sector's firms found that they could not return to their older markets. According to firms of the sector, they have had higher costs than the smaller firms in the lighter product lines because of higher overhead costs for their heavier and more capital-intensive equipment, and because of their much larger technical staffs. They have also had high expenses for advertising and public relations. These expenditures have been useful for facilitating access to the capital market— stock exchange listing, the mutual funds, and loans from the National Development Bank— and for helping firms attain the reputation for "quality" production and high technological capabilities necessary to compete in the heavier product markets. But since pricing policy in the sector attempts to recover overhead costs, these charges have often put them at a competitive disadvantage vis-à-vis the smaller firms. The smaller firms also have had lower direct costs because they have been better able to evade tax collection; the authorities have concentrated their limited collection resources on the larger firms.

Factor market imperfections related to size also hampered the smaller firms attempting to acquire the local or imported know-how necessary for more complex products. Because of reduced competition, as the sector's firms made the transition to the heavier products, they earned higher returns.

Within the heavier and more complex product lines, firms also entered new markets, and often maintained several different product lines.[24] First, there was a desire for diversification. Demand for engineering products in individual markets was relatively narrow and unstable. Because the timing of fluctuations varied for different products, firms tried to manufacture various products which, taken together over time, would constitute an adequate market. Furthermore, pioneering in the production of a product previously not made domestically usually permitted short-term monopoly profits. Other firms reacted to this demonstration of production feasibility and above-average returns by following the innovator into the new market. As a result, profits were soon depressed, and pressure was put on the pioneering firm to enter still other new markets. Such a process, in which a pioneer soon found himself surrounded by competitors whose presence stimulated further innovation, has been a major theme in the sector's development.

Entry into several product lines also avoided the pressure on marginal profits that would result if firms expanded by moving down the lower range of their demand curve in individual markets. Firms perceive these markets in terms of a downward-sloping demand curve, along which sales can be expanded only at lower unit prices. On the supply side, however, according to company officials, the technology for producing different engineering products is very similar. Because most of the sector's products are one-of-a-kind, its activity costs are similar whether the marginal product is in a new or an old product line. Most foundry, machining, and welding capacity, both in equipment and in manpower skills, is not specific to particular products. For example, capacity can be transferred from manufacture of custom-made overhead cranes to production of paper- or cement-making equipment. Usually all that a firm required to enter a new product line was

24. This is a pattern which has also been reported of other Brazilian machinery producers. See *Las Máquinas-Herramientas en el Brasil* (*La Fabricación de Maquinarias y Equipos Industriales en América Latina*, vol. 2 [New York: United Nations, 1962]), pp. 30–32.

small investments in specialized know-how, for instance, the designs of the new product. Under these conditions, firms maximized profits by allocating capacity between several product markets to avoid the declining marginal prices and profits that would occur if they expanded by selling to the lower ranges of the demand curve.

Such expansion into new markets was facilitated by the fact that, as mentioned, the sector's equipment and labor skills were in large part not specific to particular products. Moreover, new client industries often required components which had previously been supplied to other industries. For example, boiler-work products for the basic processes of heat, pressure, and filtering were often similar, whether supplied for sugar mills or for chemical and petrochemical installations. Similarly, machined components such as gears, reductors, and cylinders fit into the equipment delivered to new as well as older client industries. Consequently, entry into new markets did not mean that manufacture of the new product had to begin *de novo*.

This pattern of expansion increased the diversification of Brazilian equipment supply. It also raised marginal and total profits, which, with optimistic expectations and high plow-back rates, provided the investment resources for the sector's further growth. The know-how and production experience gained from the broader range of products, and particularly from products of increasing technical complexity, also facilitated subsequent development. This additional domestic technical capacity was especially important for management personnel—their learning and increased technical self-confidence helped them take on new products previously considered beyond domestic capabilities.

ENTRY OF THE FOREIGN FIRMS

The sector's growth and its evolution toward heavier and more complex product lines were strongly supported by entry of foreign firms in the late 1950's. Half the companies in the sector are local subsidiaries of international corporations.[25] Two are German-based,

25. Country of origin was determined by the home country where the company conducts most of its operations. The participation of American firms in this sector compares with a figure of 43% for the United States' share in total direct, foreign private investments in Brazil during the period 1955–1963 (computed from Banco do Brasil, *Relatório de 1963* [Rio de Janeiro, 1964], p. 236).

two are French, two are Japanese, two are American, one is Swiss, and one is British. These companies had previous connections with the Brazilian market through export sales and bidding in international tenders. Two of them had already established Brazilian subsidiaries for manufacture of consumer products. Most companies began studying the possibility of installing manufacturing facilities in Brazil in the years 1956–1960, and began production in the period 1958–1961.

The size of the Brazilian market and the returns it appeared to offer were the major factors attracting the foreign firms. Brazilian GNP in 1956–1960 was of the magnitude of 18–20 billion dollars.[26] This was one of the biggest markets in all the less-developed countries, and was of a scale large enough to make overseas corporations consider seriously the possibilities of a Brazilian manufacturing operation. Equally important, the economy's record of sustained, high growth rates gave promise of an even larger market in the future. Because of Brazil's persistent balance-of-payments problem during the 1950's, however, it was not possible to supply this market completely through customary export channels. As foreign-exchange shortages reduced potential sales, overseas firms began to consider the possibility of supplying this market from local manufacturing facilities. Instead of supplying the final product, they would supply only the capital and know-how from the advanced countries.

At the same time, the Brazilian government was also interested in encouraging local production of capital goods. Policymakers believed that this would alleviate balance-of-payments pressures, because foreign exchange would be required only for imported inputs instead of being required, as previously, for the entire product.[27] The government was also concerned with developing domestic-equipment production in order to promote capital formation and national development. In the early 1950's, an important public investment program had been curtailed for lack

26. *The Economic Development of Latin America in the Post-War Period* (New York: United Nations, 1964), p. 113.

27. Government policy throughout this period followed the assumption that import substitution would indeed reduce foreign-exchange demands, rather than raise them through the income-creation effect generating demands for new imports. This assumption can be questioned. See Nathaniel H. Leff and Antônio Delfim Netto, "Import Substitution, Foreign Investment, and International Disequilibrium in Brazil," *Journal of Development Studies*, 3 (April 1966), 218–233.

of foreign exchange to import needed equipment.[28] It was generally believed that future supply of imports would be inelastic with respect to domestic income, and that foreign-exchange constraints would limit investment in the future. Consequently, policymakers now gave special priority to establishment of local equipment manufacture. With these goals, the government welcomed investment by foreign capital-goods producers, for it was believed that they would make a net addition to domestic supply capacity.

Several measures were taken to improve the "investment climate" and attract foreign private investors. The government relaxed previous restrictions regarding profit remissions by foreign companies, and made direct contact with some companies to invite their investment in Brazil. These measures amounted to a removal of institutional barriers, such as fear of discrimination, which might otherwise have obstructed the flow of foreign investment to Brazil.

In addition to favorable demand conditions, foreign firms were also attracted to Brazil because of factors on the supply side which offered the prospect of high returns. Overseas investment appeared to offer an opportunity for capitalizing on the production and administrative know-how that these firms had developed in their home operations. Although this technical capacity was available to the foreign firms at zero marginal cost, Brazilian companies beginning manufacture of these products would have the expense of acquiring it through licensing agreements and production experience.[29] The foreign firms were also encouraged in their overseas ventures by the possibility of using second-hand equipment that was available relatively cheaply, so that the equipment part of their commitment could be made at a low capital cost. All the sector's foreign firms have made extensive use of used equipment which would otherwise have been scrapped as economically obsolete in their home-country plants. Such equipment, available to the firm at an opportunity cost little higher than its scrap value,

28. This was the investment program proposed by the Joint Brazil-United States Commission, whose projects were not supported by the Eisenhower administration.

29. Concerning the prospect of competition from other foreign companies who would also have know-how available at zero marginal cost, firms usually believed that the Brazilian market would be large enough to provide ample profits for all foreign firms and, indeed, often took investment by a foreign competitor as an indication that they should themselves invest in Brazil. On both points, cf. the discussion below, pp. 32–33, 35–36, on the reasons for excess capacity in the sector.

may still have a useful economic life in the conditions of a less-developed economy.[30] For example, equipment that has been scrapped for machinery of greater capital-intensity or larger optimal scale may be economic because of different relative factor prices or a smaller market size. Foreign management may also expect that even when such technology does entail high-cost production, weak domestic competition and protection from imports may still permit its use.

The opportunity of using such relatively cheap second-hand machinery was especially attractive to foreign companies, because it reduced their capital commitment in a risky environment. This is important to companies considering investment in an under-developed economy; for apart from their other uncertainties, and however favourable the existing "investment climate," management may still fear possible losses from exchange-rate depreciation, or confiscation. Had it not been possible to invest at a relatively low capital cost to the firm, probably much less foreign investment would have occurred.[31]

According to the heavy-engineering sector's foreign firms, these factors affecting the supply of foreign investment were reinforced as higher management circles in the advanced countries passed through cycles of enthusiasm concerning investment in Brazil. Such spurts of optimism spread from company to company in this industry and in others. An element of fad was also present, as the

30. The domestic firms have also made very extensive use of such machinery from the advanced countries, and almost all of their large equipment was bought second-hand, either from dealers or from firms about to scrap it. Firms have usually been careful, however, to avoid purchasing used equipment whose low productivity and high maintenance costs might make it "scrap" even under Brazilian conditions.

31. The foreign firms generally did not bring their working capital with them but relied on the local banks and suppliers. In some cases, foreign firms also built their factories with resources from the domestic economy, either from local partners or with loans from the National Development Bank. These are some of the very practices for which Brazilian nationalists have condemned direct foreign private investment. The charge is made, for instance, that the contribution by foreign investors to domestic capital formation is relatively small, consisting only of "scrap metal," while these firms draw their working capital from the local economy. At the same time, it is said that foreign companies have the unfair advantage of access under privileged terms to specialized technical know-how from the advanced countries. As suggested in the text, one reason for the relatively low capital investment by the foreign firms may be that they are making an effort to reduce their capital commitment in a risky environment. That is, whereas the domestic Brazilian firms rely heavily on second-hand equipment because of capital shortage, the foreign firms may do so because they are balancing off profit maximization against possible capital losses stemming from political factors. The political risks in turn arise out of the hostile climate created by local nationalists.

idea of establishing a Brazilian plant took on increasing respectability in management circles.[32] Moreover, one firm's decision to invest often triggered a similar decision by its competitors. Firms feared being excluded from the market by tariff protection and the advantages of an early foothold established by their rivals.[33] The Brazilian authorities played upon such fears skillfully by conducting negotiations with several firms simultaneously and by establishing deadlines, before which entrants were rewarded with special privileges and after which entrance would be possible only under less favorable conditions. Furthermore, rather than themselves making a thorough study of Brazilian market conditions, many firms accepted a competitor's decision to invest as proof of feasibility.[34]

In addition to these factors, we should note how a cumulative foreign investment boom can easily be touched off in a country like Brazil. Because of induced effects on local capital formation, investment in the economy may increase rapidly. Increased investment, in turn, may have great income-creating effects because of a relatively high investment multiplier. Consequently, domestic demand may increase rapidly, adding to the size of the market and attracting further foreign capital. In addition, the growth in foreign and domestic investment may add to the local supply

32. The sector's experience contrasts with the difficulties expected by Victor Urquidi (*The Challenge of Latin American Development* [New York, 1964], pp. 101, 122) in the coordination of government priorities with the choice of investment areas by the private sector. Urquidi posits conflict between Latin American governments and private firms, both domestic and foreign, who, he believes, will not be willing to invest in sectors accorded high priority by the government. Private firms (cf. p. 22 above) have been willing to invest in the Brazilian heavy-engineering industry, however, because the prospect of favorable market conditions created by public sector agencies answered to their own needs. As we will see below, private firms were attracted to the capital goods industry even to the extent of over-investment.

33. Cf. Lincoln Gordon's discussion of factors affecting the decisions of American firms to invest in Brazil, "Incentivos aos Investimentos Americanos no Brasil," *Revista de Administração de Emprêsas*, 1 (January-April 1962), 78–79.

34. Such investment behavior hardly appears rational in terms of short- or medium-term profit maximization, unless the market is believed large enough to afford ample profits both for the second entrant and for the firm he is following. In this case, logically the first firm should install sufficient capacity to supply the entire lucrative market. This investment behavior may be explicable, however, in terms of oligopoly behavior in which market rivals try to maintain market shares and similar growth rates vis-à-vis each other. It may also be justified in terms of a long investment horizon of large corporations that leads them to accept low immediate returns in order to establish a foothold in a market expected to grow rapidly in the future. On the latter point, cf. testimony in the hearings of the U.S. Senate Subcommittee on American Republics, *U.S. Business and Labor in Latin America* (86th Cong., 1960), chaps. I-III.

facilities for materials and components. The opportunity to rely on such suppliers is important for foreign firms, both as a source of supply free from import difficulties and because it permits them to reduce the amount of their own investment commitment.

With the entry of the foreign companies and expansion of the domestic firms, output in the sector grew very rapidly in the last half of the 1950's.[35] Equally important, production started on many new "heavy" and "technically complex" products previously considered beyond local capabilities and gave promise of accelerated expansion in the future. According to firms in the sector, a boom atmosphere developed, with high profits and "euphoric" expectations of further rapid growth and high returns. In 1959 and 1960, there were large additions to the sector's capacity, and its growth was so impressive that these years were enthusiastically described as those of "the establishment of the national heavy mechanical industry." In 1960, however, a new period in the sector's history began.

THE PERIOD 1960–1964

THE DEVELOPMENT OF EXCESS CAPACITY

After 1960, demand and output continued to grow rapidly until the slackening in aggregate Brazilian growth that began in 1963. The sector's productive capacity had grown even faster, however, so that excess capacity now developed. Excess capacity was also widespread in the entire capital goods industry by 1960, despite the large increases in national income and demand in that and preceding years.[36]

35. The ECLA study, *Basic Equipment in Brazil*, p. 63, speaks of an annual growth rate of between 10 and 15%. For the metalworking industries as a whole, most of whose output is equipment, another ECLA study presents data that indicate that the labor force grew at an annual cumulative rate of 17.2% for São Paulo State and 15.0% for all Brazil between 1955 and 1960. Value added probably grew even more rapidly because of the introduction of new products and more mechanized technology during this period. The ECLA data are presented in *Las Máquinas-Herramientas en el Brasil*, p. 20, Table 14.

36. This is stated clearly in the comments of the Banco do Estado de São Paulo on the mechanical industry in 1960 (see p. 149). For testimony on excess capacity in other equipment industries even before the 1963 slowing of aggregate growth, see "Auge y Declinación," pp. 48, 60. A discussion of the shipbuilding industry in 1962 also emphasizes the importance of excess capacity due to lack of effective demand, which was called "the fundamental problem of this industry." See the discussion in "Impacto da Indústria de Construção Naval," *Boletim da Associação Brasileira de Metais*, 19 (January 1963), 91–92.

TABLE II-5. Estimated Capacity Utilization in the Heavy-Engineering Products Sector, 1960

Product	(a) Annual estimated demand	(b) Annual estimated supply capacity	(c) Relation of estimated demand to capacity
	(Tons or sq. meters of heating surface)		(a/b) (Percent)
Pressure vessels, cyclones, large diameter tubes	7,180	16,530	43
Heat exchangers, surface condensers	100,700	62,500	161
Steam generators, direct-fired, upright furnaces	31,600	122,500	26
Metal structures and direct-fired, horizontal furnaces	11,410	53,500	21
Storage tanks	55,660	45,000	124
Electrical turbines	560	2,800	20
Electrical generators	900	1,875	48
Step-up transformers	270	1,280	21

Source: ECLA, *Basic Equipment in Brazil* (*The Manufacture of Industrial Machinery and Equipment in Latin America*, vol. 1 [New York: United Nations, 1963]), pp. 18–19, 31–33.

Table II–5 presents data on capacity utilization in the heavy-engineering products sector in 1960. These are based on the detailed estimates of demand and of supply capacity made by the ECLA mission which studied this sector in that year,[37] and reveal that as early as 1960 the sector had developed considerable excess capacity.[38] For most products, the degree of capacity utilization

37. Although ECLA's *Basic Equipment in Brazil* was published in 1963, the field work on which it is based was conducted in late 1960 (p. 1), and the estimates of supply capacity and demand relate to that year. The estimates of supply capacity are based on data from firms of the sector, and on observations by the ECLA mission. They are subject to the usual difficulties inherent in definitions of capacity. But when account is taken of the effect of imports, as discussed below, the margins of excess capacity indicated are so large that the general picture presented appears reliable.

38. The ECLA study also contained estimates for the supply of equipment used in the cement and paper industries (pp. 46, 53). For the cement industry, it estimated 14% under-capacity in 1962 and, for the paper industry, 10% excess capacity in 1961–1965. Unlike the statistics cited in the text, however, these figures are estimates for future years rather than observed conditions. Moreover, these figures are based on projections of demand in which it was assumed that the economy would continue to grow at rates similar to those of the booming late-1950's, while possible increases in supply capacity were not fully taken into account. On both counts, these projections were disproved by events, and so these estimates are not included in Table II-5.

was between approximately 20 and 50 percent. Heat-exchangers and metal tanks appear to be exceptions to this pattern, but domestic supply capacity for these products was actually much greater than Table II–5 indicates. The ECLA mission did not include in its figures the capacity of many smaller companies, of the 50- to 200-employee size, which, firms in the sector testify, have been quite capable of participating in the market for lighter and less complex products, either directly or as subcontractors. Adding these firms to estimates of domestic supply would have shown that the pressure on capacity for these products was more illusory than real.[39] In fact, data available on capacity and actual output of metal tanks for two companies within the sector indicate that in these products, too, there was considerable excess capacity in 1960 and subsequently.[40]

More generally, the data in Table II–5 seriously understate the extent of excess capacity in all products, for the figures on size of market do not take account of the large portion of demand which was supplied by importation rather than by domestic producers. Approximately 25 percent of aggregate Brazilian equipment supply has come from imports. In the sector under study here the percentage has been much higher, approximately 45 percent, because heavy-equipment projects have generally been supplied with foreign credits, which have been crucial in maintaining imports.[41] Applying this import coefficient to the data on demand in Table II–5, in order to subtract the portion of the market which was in reality supplied by imports, would increase the degree of domestic capacity under-utilization to even higher levels.

CAUSES OF THE EXCESS CAPACITY

The sector's excess capacity did not stem from some of the factors that are often associated with capacity under-utilization in less-developed countries—for example, technological indivisibilities

39. In 1963 there were approximately 37 smaller firms, mostly in the 50- to 200-employee range, with a total work-force of approximately 4,300, producing such metal structures. Data are from a trade publication, *Anuário BANAS, Máquinas e Ferramentas, 1963* (São Paulo, 1964).

40. In 1960, the capacity of one company in the sector, Fichet & Schwartz-Haumont, was estimated at 10,000 tons output of storage tanks per year (ECLA, *Basic Equipment in Brazil*, p. 18), but actual output was 5,300 tons in 1960 and 6,144 tons in 1961 (*Anuário BANAS*, p. 138). Similarly, capacity of another firm, Santa Matilda, was rated in 1960 at 6,000 tons annually. Its actual production was: 1960, 275 tons; 1961, 2,178 tons; 1962, 2,543 tons (*Anuário BANAS*, p. 141).

41. On these points, see Chap. VI.

or input bottlenecks. Suspension of supply from imports did not play a role in this case, for by 1960 more than 90 percent of Brazilian consumption of steel plate and bars, the sector's principal raw material, was supplied domestically.[42] According to the sector's firms, given the existence of effective demand in their product market, inputs such as steel, nonferrous metals, and skilled labor were readily available without supply constraints. Furthermore, unlike the situation in electricity generation or in some chemical industries, the sector's technology does not entail large capital indivisibilities, such that over a large range, minimum-cost production may be achieved with substantial under-utilized capacity. Rather, its capacity is expanded by adding one machine tool after another, along a relatively continuous production function.[43] There are also no rigid complementarities between machines, so that adding one would require adding other equipment which, taken together, might amount to a sizeable indivisibility.

Rather, the sector's excess capacity seems to be a case of sectoral over-building which occurred because of the way firms made their investment plans. Reacting to the favorable market conditions and expectations generated in the earlier period, the older firms and new entrants installed more capacity than the market could absorb over the short or medium term.

First, firms overestimated the size of the market. They approached the question of entrance to the sector, or expansion of existing capacity, with the "euphoria"—as they describe it—created by the boom of the late 1950's. They expected the economy to continue its previous high growth rates, and they added to their demand projections an intuitive idea of a high income-elasticity of demand for equipment. As they put it: the market for capital goods was sure to grow especially rapidly in the course of economic development. In addition to growth in the aggregate demand for equipment, they also expected that domestic producers would sharply increase their share of the market through replacement of supplies previously imported. To these intuitions, the domestic companies also added an upward bias due to their enthusiasm

---

42. "Auge'y Declinación," p. 45, Table 27.
43. Information is from firms in the sector. The only relatively large and indivisible machines used in the sector are a 120-inch horizontal lathe and a 35-foot boring mill.

concerning the prospects for capital goods production in Brazil.

The foreign company executives studying the potentialities of the Brazilian market also shared the general optimism. Their enthusiasm concerning Brazil's economic prospects was especially important because of the way in which foreign firms often made their investment decisions. In describing this process, Lincoln Gordon draws an explicit contrast between "rational" decision-making and the "more subjective" approach actually taken: "Theoretically, he [the foreign investor] takes the decision to invest based on rational calculations, beginning with scientific market research and forecasts of potential volume of sales, costs, and prices . . . In practice, however, this is usually not the case with American companies operating in underdeveloped countries. The same rational ideal may be desired, but usually there are no statistics for systematic market research . . . As a result, the real decision-making process is more subjective and depends on the impressions of the major executives."[44]

These optimistic intuitions were reinforced by the market studies that were conducted by the domestic and foreign firms.[45] The standard technique of market research in Brazil has been to judge the size of the domestic market for a given product by the volume of its imports.[46] As applied to capital goods, this procedure gave a seriously misleading picture, exaggerating the size of the market for domestically produced goods and the possibilities for import substitution.

Most Brazilian capital goods imports have been financed by foreign resources. Indeed, more than 80 percent of the 2,700 million dollars worth of equipment imported by Brazil during the period 1957–1963 was financed by foreign savings, either suppliers'

44. Gordon, "Incentivos aos Investimentos Americanos," pp. 83–84 (my translation). Gordon's observations were limited to American firms, but my own interviews indicate a similar pattern for the other foreign firms, which generally consider the American firms as paragons of scientific business administration.

45. After interviewing the domestic and foreign firms in the sector about the way in which they planned their investments, I sometimes had the impression that decisions in the sector followed Parkinson's suggestion that the biggest questions get the least amount of careful consideration. (See C. Northcote Parkinson, *Parkinson's Law* [London, 1957], pp. 63ff.) The major decisions about entering the sector or expanding capacity seem often to have been made on the basis of general impressions and intuition. The less important, implementing plans were made much more carefully.

46. This technique was apparently not penalized in many other industries—e.g., consumer durables—because a high income-elasticity of demand and rapidly growing national income provided an adequate market, at least until the post-1962 economic slowdown.

credits or direct foreign investment.[47] Hence these imports did not indicate effective demand for equipment, supported by the domestic resources necessary to finance purchase of investment goods. Rather, they reflected nothing more than market preferences, which could be sustained in this case by the availability of foreign resources tied to purchase of imported equipment. Because so large a portion of "demand" for imported equipment existed only because of this foreign saving, the volume of imports exaggerated the extent of the domestic resources actually allocated to purchase of investment goods.[48] Not correcting for this distortion, however, firms took the high level of imports as evidence of a large market for their products, and installed capacity in excess of the market's real possibilities.[49]

Firms also underestimated the growth in the sector's capacity that was preceeding concurrently with their own investment plans. The advent of the foreign firms and the opening of new sources of capital for the domestic firms permitted much faster rates of capacity expansion than had previously been possible. Until the mid-1950's, the sector's rate of expansion had been constrained by the availability of investment resources from profit reinvestment within the domestic firms. The development of new sources of outside capital now permitted a shift in the parameters affecting the sector's capacity growth. In making their individual investment

47. Data were kindly supplied by the Research Division of SUMOC.

48. This distortion did not occur in using import levels to judge the size of the market for consumer goods. By a government decision, foreign suppliers' credits were reserved almost exclusively for capital goods imports.

49. This may have occurred either because of a simple error or because the data on the very high percentage of equipment imports financed by foreign resources are not generally accessible. These data are not generally available, and I was given access to this information by the Brazilian monetary authority only upon the assurance that I was working on a scholarly project, "without commercial purposes." As we will see below, however, the government agency planning the sector's growth, which *did* have access to these data, made the same mistake. This suggests that the fault lay in the application of the standard market research technique in a situation where it gave seriously misleading results. Alternatively, it might be thought that the error lay in overestimating the amount of credits that would be available to finance purchase of domestically produced equipment. This does not appear likely, however. For reasons discussed in Chap. VI, the Brazilian National Development Bank consistently refused to finance domestic equipment purchases. Furthermore, it does not seem likely that investors in the sector expected untied foreign credits to be available to finance their sales. Such foreign credits have been supplied largely by foreign government agencies such as the American EXIMBANK. As a matter of policy, they have almost always linked their credit to purchases of equipment from their home countries, presumably because the distortion this introduces in the product market permits higher returns for their national producers.

plans, however, firms may not have been fully aware of other companies' expansion. Even to the extent that companies did know about each other's projects, it was generally believed, for the reasons cited, that there was an ample market for all. Moreover, the alternatives to rapid individual expansion would have been to leave the market or to come to an agreement with other firms to limit entry and capacity expansion. With the ebullient expectations of the late 1950's, and with the commitment of the domestic firms to the heavy-engineering sector and participation in its growth, such an agreement would have been unthinkable.[50] Entry by the powerful foreign firms posed the prospect of increasing competitive pressures most clearly. Even so, when approached by foreign bidders, all the domestic firms chose to take their competitive chances rather than sell out.[51]

The way in which the foreign firms made their investment decisions also contributed to a disproportionately rapid increase in the sector's capacity. First, the practice of establishing a Brazilian plant because a competitor was doing so and the "bunching" of investment decisions in response to a government deadline contributed to a sharp increase in capacity within a relatively short period.[52] "Bunching" of foreign investment occurred in two ways. Many firms entered the market at the same time to gain the advantages of an early foothold and duty-free treatment for their equipment imports. Within the individual firms, investment plans were also made on a larger scale than would otherwise have been justified, in order to "get under the wire" of the government deadline and install the plant under relatively favorable conditions.[53]

The foreign firms also exaggerated their ability to compete successfully with local firms and hence overestimated their indi-

50. As noted in Chap. VII, as late as 1964, despite excess capacity and pressure on margins, the domestic firms refused, because of long-term expectations, to leave the sector or enter into mergers reducing capacity.

51. In the middle 1950's, two domestic firms had sold out to foreign companies, but this was before the subsequent extremely rapid growth and the expectations it created. Furthermore, these may have been special cases. One seller had no heir to continue his family firm. The other was a São Paulo Polytechnic graduate who preferred to found a technical school.

52. See n. 34 above.

53. A similar situation of excess capacity as a result of foreign firms "bunching" their investment because of a government deadline seems to have occurred also in Argentina. See David Felix, "Import Substituting Industrialization and Industrial Exporting in Argentina," mimeographed (Instituto Torquato di Tella, Buenos Aires, September 1964), p. 40.

vidual markets. The foreign firms often assumed that on the basis of their size, and especially their administrative and technical know-how, they would be able to dominate the local market. This did not prove to be the case.

The domestic firms were usually able to compete effectively using their know-how, obtained both from local sources and through licensing agreements with other overseas firms. Moreover, the foreign firms often had special disadvantages of their own. Their larger size and their expatriate managerial and technical staffs contributed to higher unit overhead costs.[54] Because they employed a "cost plus" pricing policy which attempted to recover overhead costs in the markup, this often placed them at a competitive price disadvantage. Furthermore, because of the foreign firms' reluctance (stemming from fears about the exchange-rate and political conditions) to increase their capital commitment in Brazil, they usually did not bring with them sufficient working capital to provide substantial suppliers' credits to local clients. Hence they were sometimes at a competitive disadvantage vis-à-vis domestic firms, which from their accumulated reserves could offer sufficient finance to maintain sales. Finally, some foreign firms encountered special administrative problems, caused alternatively by overly rigid or overly flexible bureaucratic control of the local subsidiary. Loose control sometimes permitted local mismanagement—including one episode of serious embezzling. Overly rigid bureaucratic structure sometimes prevented firms from adjusting to local conditions—for example, in adapting their product to the Brazilian market's general preferences for a product lower in quality and lower in price than customary in the advanced countries.[55]

54. John C. Shearer, in his study of manpower practices by American subsidiaries in Brazil (*High-Level Manpower in Overseas Subsidiaries* [Princeton, 1960], pp. 117, 124–132), tells of American firms employing expatriates at a cost four times that of equivalent manpower from domestic sources. To a lesser degree, the other foreign firms also made extensive use of expensive expatriates.

55. Concerning this point, see the discussion in Chap. V. This inflexibility may sometimes be rational from the view of the international corporation as a whole. The home office may not want to sacrifice its worldwide reputation and market for high-quality production in order to increase sales in the relatively small Brazilian market. The foreign firms have generally *not* been inflexible in adjusting their production technology to local conditions—e.g., different relative factor-prices. In my interviews, I was often given explanations that under Brazilian conditions it is economical to use techniques more labor-intensive than in the advanced countries.

Because of these factors, when field investigation of the sector was undertaken in 1964, the foreign rather than the domestic firms were bearing a disproportionate share of its excess capacity and low profit margins. In boiler products, one prominent international company had closed its plant and gone into reorganization at the same time as some local firms were doing well enough to expand capacity. In papermaking equipment, local firms had a better profit performance than a foreign firm with worldwide reputation. A similar situation generally prevailed in the sector's other product lines.

This demonstration of the domestic firms' competitive ability, however, came only after the foreign firms had already installed their capacity. Because of their earlier overestimation of their market share, they did not modify their investment plans to take cognizance of the local firms' expansion, even to the extent that they were aware of it. And, for their own reasons, the domestic firms also underestimated or refused to adjust to growth of capacity occurring simultaneously with their own investment plans. Consequently, sectoral over-building could develop.

We should note that this resource misallocation did not arise because of any lack of "planning" or government coordination of market decisions; it was caused rather by technically poor planning. Through the Executive Group for the Mechanical Industry (GEIMAPE), the government played an active role in the sector's growth; its approval was necessary for entry by foreign firms and for most capacity expansion by domestic companies. Furthermore, through its control of import licences, it had the policy instrument to make its wishes felt directly on individual investment plans.

The planning agency, however, was also carried away by the general optimism and overestimation of the size of the market for domestically produced equipment. Although it did have access to the statistics showing the very large percentage of equipment imports financed by foreign resources, it apparently made the mistake of confounding the volume of imports with the effective demand for domestically produced capital goods. This standard market-research technique had not led to manifest error in planning capacity for other industries—for example, automobiles.[56] Appa-

56. A similar problem did develop, however, with heavy trucks, an investment good previously imported with foreign suppliers' credits.

rently it was not realized that the demand for investment goods had to be supported by domestic savings and/or untied foreign credits, which were not forthcoming. The planners may also have overestimated the size of the market because of the ideological belief, widely held among Brazilian economists and policymakers, that demand for capital goods had been constrained by heavy dependence on overseas supply for most equipment needs.[57] According to this view, ample *ex ante* domestic demand for equipment existed, but had been repressed by the difficulties of procuring sufficient supply from importation. Hence excess capacity in domestic capital goods production hardly appeared as a real possibility: the contrary situation appeared more likely.[58] Consequently the government did not restrict the growth of capacity in the sector.[59]

SUBSEQUENT GROWTH, 1960–1964

After 1960, according to company officials, although excess capacity and intense competition put pressure on profits, demand and output in the sector continued to expand rapidly until the economic slowdown that began in 1963. Output figures for the sector are not available, but Table II–6 presents estimates for the capital goods industry as a whole. These are shown alongside data on the annual percentage increase of GNP in these years.

Because of excess capacity, some investment projects by potential

57. In Chap. IX, the importance of import supply constraints on Brazilian capital formation is questioned.

58. In support of this interpretation, we can note that, perhaps because of a blindspot introduced by ideology, the ECLA report on this sector also made no mention of the capacity under-utilization which its data indicate.

59. Other factors also contributed to the government's willingness to permit the sector's rapid expansion of capacity. Government officials have complained that the heterogeneity of the many different types of capital goods made their tasks intrinsically more difficult than that of agencies planning capacity for more homogeneous products, e.g., tons of flat steel or numbers of passenger cars. Furthermore, in the case of foreign firms presenting investment projects strictly linked to this sector, the opportunity cost to Brazil of these investment resources was low, so that the government hesitated to deny approval. The main factors, however, seem to be those cited in the text, with a further note that the goals of the planning agency did not always coincide with profit maximization for the sector's firms. Although there was apparently no deliberate effort to create excess capacity in the sector and put downward pressure on capital goods prices and profits, the government undoubtedly preferred to err with an upward bias, leaving the firms temporarily with excess capacity, rather than err on the downward side, leaving the economy with inelastic capital goods supply.

TABLE II-6. Estimated Increase in Output of
Mechanical Equipment and in GNP, 1960–1963
(Percent)

Year	Equipment output	GNP
1960	14.0	6.7
1961	14.0	7.3
1962	20.0	5.4
1963	2.6	1.6

Sources: Estimates of GNP increases are from FGV.
Estimates of equipment output are from IBRD,
"Manufacturing Industry" ("Current Economic
Position and Prospects of Brazil," vol. 5, mimeo-
graphed [Washington, D.C., February 1965]),
Annex 1, p. 2.

new entrants were canceled after 1961.[60] Nevertheless, productive
capacity in the sector as a whole continued to expand through 1963
and 1964. Some investment projects begun a year or more earlier
were now being completed with a lag. Moreover, despite the
conditions of the sector, some better-managed companies were
able to expand by increasing their market share at the expense of
other firms. Furthermore, most of the excess capacity was held by
a few large firms, and was experienced by other companies mainly
as a competitive pressure constraining profits below previous boom
levels, but still sufficient to justify positive net investment. Finally,
favorable expectations concerning the future continued to be
maintained. The ECLA report concerning the sector's prospects
was also interpreted to support continued long-term optimism.[61]

60. The specific projects of which I learned involved foreign companies in heavy electrical
equipment and papermaking equipment. Quite possibly, however, other investment plans
were also canceled at this time. Several other foreign companies, some with no Brazilian
manufacturing subsidiary and some producing in other markets (e.g., metallurgical products
and consumer durables), were known to be considering investment in the heavy-engineering
sector, and probably would have proceeded under favorable market conditions.
61. The study was interpreted rather uncritically, and attention was focused on its
projections of demand, without due consideration to their underlying assumptions. The
ECLA study illustrates the limitations of sectoral planning without complementary macro-
analysis and effective policies for aggregate growth. The study was based upon projections
of demand from the sector's client industries. From these followed the whole planning effort,
involving considerable work and analysis. These projections, however, followed the assumption that aggregate income would increase at boom rates similar to those of the late 1950's.
When this did not occur, the sectoral plan lost its validity.

As a result, the situation of capacity over-building was intensified, and in 1964 the heavy-engineering sector presented a picture of development on the supply side to the point of considerable redundant resources. Under these conditions, output can respond relatively easily to increases in demand, and future growth of the industry is largely a function of its effective demand. In Chapters V and VI, we will consider the extent to which—even apart from the recent slackening in aggregate Brazilian growth—demand for equipment can be expected to grow dynamically enough to generate vigorous growth in the capital goods industry.

This picture of elastic supply possibilities is essentially the same as we had of the sector's earlier growth: namely, that factor supply has been relatively elastic to derived demands, so that output could respond to favorable market conditions. Domestic firms were able to grow with capital attracted from elsewhere in the economy and with profits generated from past production and reinvested in the sector. Entry of the foreign firms with their resources was another case of factor supply responding to demand in the product market, for size of the local market was the main attraction that brought these companies to Brazil. In the next chapter, we turn to a detailed consideration of another input whose supply has affected the sector's ability to respond elastically to demand—skilled and technically educated manpower.

III

LABOR

Brazilian industrialization has proceeded very rapidly despite an industrial work-force with relatively poor educational preparation. Between 1947 and 1961, industrial output grew at an annual cumulative rate of 9.6 percent in spite of an overall illiteracy rate of 50 percent and many quantitative and qualitative deficiencies common to education in a less-developed economy.[1] Even in São Paulo State, the area of greatest industrial growth and highest income levels, only 73 percent of the male cohort aged 16–17 was literate in 1950.[2] In this chapter, we will focus on the ways in which problems of education and supply of skilled labor for development were dealt with.

The heavy-equipment sector is well suited to be a case study for such analysis. Its skill requirements for bench labor are among the highest in the Brazilian economy. The sector's demands for engineers are also high; and at the same time, it has required capabilities—such as training in the fields of mechanical and electrical engineering—which are new for Brazilian engineers. Not only was this sector able to grow at high rates despite these manpower requirements, but it did so in the midst of a generally expanding pressure on skilled manpower resources. During this period, the output of the entire Brazilian metalworking industry, notably the automotive and consumer-durables producers, was also expanding at annual rates of 10 percent and over. Thus in filling its manpower needs in the mechanical trades, the heavy-engineering products sector had to compete with other industries for the same scarce skills. Because supply of educated and skilled

1. For a good overview of the inadequacies of Brazilian education, see Paulo de Assis Ribeiro, "A Educação e o Planejamento," *Revista Brasileira de Economia*, 14 (December 1964). Despite the historical record of high sustained rates of economic growth achieved in the midst of a poor educational situation, some writers have persisted in suggesting that education has been a "bottleneck" to economic development in Brazil. Cf., e.g., Werner Baer, *Industrialization and Economic Development in Brazil* (Homewood, Ill., 1965), pp. 187–190.

2. Robert J. Havighurst and J. Roberto Moreira, *Society and Education in Brazil* (Pittsburgh, 1965), p. 2.

labor is sometimes considered so inelastic as to constitute a serious barrier to "big pushes" in development,[3] the Brazilian experience is also interesting from the viewpoint of general development policy.

This chapter will first deal with the sector's demands for technically educated and highly skilled manpower, and will then examine the various means by which training was supplied and how its costs and returns were allocated. Since the picture that emerges from the discussion is complex, let us anticipate its major themes. There have been large increases in the supply of the engineers and skilled workers used in the sector. At the same time, however, because demand for this manpower was also expanding very rapidly, scarcity conditions have prevailed, reflected in large quasi-rents and high relative wages for these skills. Nevertheless, for reasons we will consider, under-investment in the supply of trained personnel has not been a serious problem for the sector's expansion.

THE DEMAND FOR SKILLED AND EDUCATED LABOR

SKILLED BENCH WORKERS

Skilled workers constitute a relatively high percentage of the sector's labor force. We get some idea of the high skill coefficient from Table III–1, which shows the percentage of skilled workers for various São Paulo industries in 1962.[4] As the data indicate, skilled-worker coefficients are higher in heavy-engineering products than in other lines, except for craft industries such as printing and jewelry-making.

More important than the percentage of personnel within the broad category of "skilled workers," the sector's firms generally have skill requirements which are unusually high for the Brazilian

3. For a statement of this argument, see J. Marcus Fleming, "External Economies and the Doctrine of Balanced Growth," *Economic Journal* (June 1955), reprinted in *The Economics of Underdevelopment*, ed. A. N. Agarwala and S. P. Singh (Bombay, 1961), pp. 280–283, 293.

4. The definition of "skilled workers" in each industry follows the classification procedures developed by the SENAI in the course of its manpower surveys since the early 1940's. Its classification distinguishes skilled (*qualificados*), semiskilled (*semiqualificados*), and unskilled workers (*operários braçais*) in the factory work-force. I have here used the category *qualificados*. The São Paulo classifications may sometimes differ from what might be indicated by the Standard International Classification of Occupations, but I believe that as used by the SENAI's professional personnel, they are internally consistent enough to permit the comparison made in the text.

TABLE III-1. Skilled Workers as a Percentage of Total Labor Force in Industries of São Paulo State, 1962–1963

Industry	Percent
Heavy-engineering products	38
All-industry average	20
Mechanical (series production)	27
Textiles	7
Chemical	10
Food	13
Paper	8.
Printing	39
Jewelry-making	77

Sources: Data on heavy-engineering products were supplied by companies of the sector. Data for the other industries are from the SENAI 1962–1963 manpower survey of São Paulo industrial establishments, as reported in *Relatório do SENAI de São Paulo* (São Paulo, 1964), p. 6.

mechanical trades.[5] Machining operations must sometimes be held to tolerances of a thousandth of an inch. Welding must be of a quality able to withstand pressures of up to 240 pounds per square inch and capable of passing X-ray tests. Coil winding for electrical generators must conform to rigid standards, for errors can cause an entire generator to burn up. In all of these operations, output must conform to close specifications to avoid the serious physical danger and economic losses that might result from imperfect functioning of the goods produced.

In addition to unusually high skill levels, the sector makes other special demands on its workers. As producers of custom-made engineering products, the sector's firms fabricate a variety of nonstandardized products, and they can rarely use mass production methods. Consequently, few jobs can be broken down into small, repetitive steps which workers can easily learn. For example, much machining is done with individual setups and without the help of pre-set jigs that would lessen the demands on the machinist. Furthermore, because of the lack of product specialization, job requirements often vary, so that workers must be able to move

5. The material that follows is based on interviews with personnel directors and foremen within the firms of the sector.

flexibly within their trade. Workers above the semiskilled level must also be able to read the designs that communicate the technical specifications for individual components. And, because the work flow is not guided by an assembly line or by the machine itself, many workers must be capable of independence in their judgment and work rhythm. Thus, in high skill requirements, in capacity for flexibility, and in ability to read designs, workers must meet demands which in many other industries are required only for a few maintenance specialists.

To meet these standards, three to four years of formal education are generally required for bench workers in the sector.[6] This has been sufficient for preparing most workers to understand work instructions, assimilate requisite skills, and learn to read designs and measuring instruments.

Foremen (*mestres*) are another important element in the sector's demand for skilled personnel. Not only do they function as the factory force's supervisors and technical instructors, but they also constitute the communications link between higher management and the production process. Foremen are generally workers with several years' experience who have demonstrated a capacity for leadership, and who have the technical knowledge necessary to direct the work process and instruct workers when production problems arise. For these purposes, five to six years of formal education have usually been enough preparation. In some cases, even less formal education has sufficed. In one factory of 500 workers, for example, technical direction of the work-force rested on the shoulders of five foremen whose formal education totalled fourteen years.

ENGINEERS

In discussing the sector's demands for engineers, we should first point out some important qualitative aspects. The engineering specialities that the sector requires—mechanical and electrical engineering—are relatively new to Brazil. As recently as the early 1950's, course offerings in these fields and students wanting to study them were relatively rare. Consequently the sector's growth has depended on a capacity for change in both the engineering schools and the students. Furthermore, many of the technical jobs

6. See n. 5 above.

within the sector require a close physical connection between the engineer and the production process. In Brazil, as in many other less-developed countries, the engineering tradition has emphasized project design and office work rather than "dirty hand" production activities.

The sector's quantitative requirements for engineers are also among the highest in the Brazilian economy. The measure of demand used in the ratio of engineers employed to the total work force.[7] The coefficient for this sector is 2.2 percent.[8] Some of the foreign firms, especially those producing electrical equipment, have coefficients as high as 3 percent, whereas other firms, especially some of the domestic firms, make do with coefficients as low as 1.3

TABLE III-2. Engineers as a Percentage of the Total Labor Force in São Paulo Industries, 1963

Industry	Percent
Heavy-engineering products	2.20
All-industry average	0.04
Construction	1.50
Textile	0.02
Chemical and pharmaceutical	0.52
Mechanical (series production)	0.54

Source: Unpublished material from the SENAI manpower surveys, kindly made available by Dr. Italo Bologna of the São Paulo Confederação das Indústrias.

percent. As Table III-2 indicates, these coefficients are the highest in São Paulo industry and are four times higher than the coefficient for the São Paulo mechanical industry as a whole.

Going behind these aggregate coefficients, we can discuss the allocation of engineers to different functions. Approximately one fifth of the firms' engineering manpower is used in administration; one third works in project design; another third works in the direct supervision of production; and one fifth is used in sales and purchasing.[9] The figures point out the importance of administration and of sales and purchasing, which between them account for

7. Cf. National Science Foundation, *The Long Range Demand for Scientific and Technical Personnel: A Methodological Study* (Washington, D.C., 1962), pp. 1-6.
8. Data are from questionnaire material supplied by firms of the sector.
9. The material on demand for and allocation of engineers was supplied by firms of the sector.

TABLE III-3. Functional Allocation of Engineers in the U.S. Machinery Industry, 1960, and in the Brazilian Heavy-Engineering Sector, 1963 (Percent)

Function	Brazilian heavy-engineering sector	U.S. machinery industry
Administration	20	9
Production	30	34
Projects and development	30	38
Sales, purchasing, other	20	19

Sources: U.S. data are from National Science Foundation, *The Long Range Demand for Scientific and Technical Personnel, A Methodological Study*, (Washington, D.C., 1962), Tables A-1, A-2, A-3, A-9, A-19; National Science Foundation, *Scientific-Technical Personnel in Industry 1960* (Washington, D.C., 1961), Table A-7. Brazilian data are from questionnaires completed by firms in the sector.

approximately 40 percent of the demand for engineers. Table III–3 compares the use of engineers in the American machinery industry with that in this sector. The percentages are broadly similar, though the sector appears to use relatively more engineers in administration, and fewer in research and development and in production, than does the American machinery industry.

"EDUCATIONAL SAVING"

Although the sector's requirements are very high in comparison with other Brazilian industries, the firms use considerably lower educational inputs than companies making the same products in the advanced countries. Educational levels in the sector's work force are lower both in terms of the shop workers' formal schooling and in terms of the input of engineers. Despite educational levels lower than in the advanced countries, productivity of the Brazilian workers, when similar capital equipment is provided, is similar to productivity of the workers in the advanced countries.[10] Hence the

10. ECLA, *Basic Equipment in Brazil* (*The Manufacture of Industrial Machinery and Equipment in Brazil*, vol. 1 [New York: United Nations, 1963]), pp. 60–62. Mordechai E. Kreinin reports a similar finding in a broader study which compared labor productivity of American firms with plants producing the same products under similar capital and scale conditions overseas. See his "Comparative Labor Effectiveness and the Leontief Scarce-Factor Paradox," *American Economic Review*, 55 (March 1965), 131–140. In this article, data from 76 firms comparing worker productivity in their U.S. and their Latin American operations showed a median worker productivity of approximately 77% of American worker-productivity standards, despite the much lower median education per worker in Latin America (p. 137,

sector's practices in employing lower levels of educational inputs for producing the same output can be called "educational saving."

SHOP WORKERS

According to the sector's foreign company managers, the educational coefficients noted above, three to four years' schooling for skilled workers and five to six years for foremen, are considerably lower than those customary in the advanced countries. In the home factories of the European and Japanese companies, workers in the same jobs usually have six to eight years of formal schooling, and foremen have eight to ten. In the home plants of the sector's American companies, these tasks are usually performed by people with even more formal education, ten to twelve years of school.[11]

Because Brazilian workers are generally equipped with inferior equipment, their actual productivity is lower than in the advanced countries. But this difference is more than offset by their much lower wages, so that the productivity/wage ratio is higher in Brazil than in the advanced countries. In terms of the ratio of total factor productivity to total factor costs, the sector also makes a good showing. Despite its lower stocks of both human and physical capital as compared with producers in the advanced countries, the sector's final product prices are generally competitive with world market levels.[12] Furthermore, the sector's firms report that their relatively unschooled work-force does not lack flexibility. As noted in the previous chapter, during the 1950's firms made a major transition toward heavier and more complex products. Workers adjusted easily to these changes, which usually required adaptation to more rigorous tolerances and to new fabricating equipment. Indeed, the sector's foreign plant managers sometimes compare disparagingly the rigidity and resistance to change of European workers with the greater adaptability of Brazilian personnel.

The marked differences in formal education between the Brazilian workers and their counterparts in the advanced countries,

---

Table 3). Moreover, of this difference in productivity, only about half was attributed to differences in worker education and inadequate training as opposed to other factors (p. 137, Table 4).

11. This is also borne out by data in the U.S. Census. See Bureau of Census, *Occupational Characteristics, U.S. Census of Population, 1960* (Washington, D.C., 1964), pp. 118–120.

12. ECLA, *Basic Equipment in Brazil*, pp. 60–62.

without any proportionate productivity increases arising from the latter's higher education, suggest that the greater schooling input in the advanced countries may result less from factors on the demand side, related to higher productivity of workers with more education, than from conditions affecting the supply of education in the work-force.[13]

The Brazilian firms demand labor with a minimum of formal schooling, enough to give functional literacy, and this, along with native intelligence and psychomotor capacities, prepares workers for their future tasks. Aptitude and preparation tests are usually used to select workers with sufficient abilities for subsequent assimilation of skills and technical knowledge. Although individual Brazilian firms could hire personnel with educational attainments as high as in the advanced countries, they do not believe that their higher productivity would be sufficient to justify increased costs. In the advanced countries, however, higher income levels and expenditure on education have created a population of greater formal-education attainment. As supply of personnel with higher educational levels has increased relative to other labor grades, employers in the developed countries have been able to raise educational standards in their hiring practices without proportionate cost increases. Thus, although the work-force has more formal schooling, this may not be strictly related to job requirements or proportionately increased productivity of better educated personnel.

We should also note that in a less-developed country, formal education above a minimum level may be less strictly related to worker capabilities than in a developed country. In the advanced countries, where access to education may be much more widespread than in a poor country, the school system performs a sifting function, screening individuals of intelligence, ability, and motivation as they pass through successively higher educational levels. If there is relatively equal access to the system, ability and higher educational attainment may be closely correlated. Because of unequal access to the educational system in many less-developed countries, however, many individuals of ability and motivation may not have the opportunity to enter this selective mechanism. Consequently, the correlation between educational attainment

13. For a similar suggestion, see Gary Becker, "Investment in Human Capital: A Theoretical Analysis," *Journal of Political Economy*, 70, pt. 2 (October 1962), 40.

and intrinsic capabilities is likely to be much lower, and it is far more probable that individuals without higher education may indeed have real ability. With their native intelligence alone, such people may be able to assimilate skills and further knowledge, and perform at relatively high productivity levels.[14]

ENGINEERS

Firms in the sector also employ fewer engineers than companies producing the same products in the advanced countries. The Brazilian companies employ 2.2 graduate engineers per 100 employees. By contrast, firms in the American machinery and electrical equipment industries employ 5.7 engineers per 100 employees.[15] Because the relevant comparison for present purposes is in terms of engineer inputs per unit of output, we should correct the Brazilian figure upward to reflect the lower productivity of the Brazilian work-force, attributable to their inferior production equipment. According to the American firms of the sector, productivity of the Brazilian personnel is approximately 75 percent of American levels. Hence the Brazilian engineer coefficient, expressed in terms of employees of comparable output, is approximately 2.9. This still leaves the input of engineers in the Brazilian sector less than half of that in the American industry.[16]

This disparity in engineer coefficients implies that demand for engineers has a degree of flexibility and is not strictly determined by technology. If manpower requirements were rigidly related to technical conditions, we might expect the Brazilian engineer

14. It might be thought that such educational saving has been possible only because the skilled industrial work-force has consisted of individuals of unusually high intrinsic aptitude and intelligence, who make up but a small fraction of the population. The literature on the subject suggests, however, that the "pool of ability" is much larger than is generally believed. Cf. P. de Wolff and K. Harnquist, "Reserves of Ability: Size and Distribution," in *Ability and Educational Opportunity*, ed. A. H. Halsey· (Paris: OECD, 1961); and Dael Wolfle, *America's Resources of Specialized Talent* (New York, 1954), pp. 312–314.

15. Computed from: National Science Foundation, *The Long Range Demand*, Tables A-1, A-3, A-9; National Science Foundation, *Scientific-Technical Personnel in Industry 1960* (Washington, D.C., 1961) Table A-13.

16. In reality, the American engineer input for this sector of heavy-engineering products may be even higher, and the disparity with the Brazilian coefficient even greater, for the figure cited refers to the American machinery industry as a whole, including series-made products. Table III-2 above shows an engineer coefficient for Brazilian heavy-engineering products much higher than for the machinery industry as a whole. Neither the United States Occupational Census, the National Science Foundation, nor the Engineering Joint Council report data sufficiently disaggregated to calculate an engineer coefficient for the American heavy-engineering products sector alone.

coefficients to be identical with those of the American sector. If there were similar production technology in both countries, and if there were no great economies of scale, marginal physical productivity of engineers in the same sector would be similar in the two countries. If, furthermore, final product prices were similar, marginal value productivity would also be the same. Hence it might be expected that the demand curves for engineers and engineer coefficients for the same sector in the different countries would likewise be similar. Reviewing the applicability of these conditions, we can say that the second and third are fulfilled. The first condition does not hold completely, for the Brazilian firms use older and less automatic equipment than American firms. This, however, might often increase the demand for engineers, for more personnel are needed to deal with the operation and maintenance problems created by secondhand and manually operated equipment. Such a rigid "manpower requirements" approach to the demand for engineers would imply zero elasticity of substitution in production between this grade of labor and other inputs. Our data indicate, however, that the sector's production function has permitted a range of substitution between engineers and other inputs. We can gain some insight into this process by considering how firms approach the question of hiring engineering personnel.[17]

As in many other less-developed countries, engineers' salaries in Brazil are very high relative to other wages. Although the absolute level of engineers' salaries is lower than in the United States, it appears very high to Brazilian employers, and they make every effort to economize in the use of engineers. Firms have done this in two ways. First, they have eliminated some jobs (by doing less work in research and development and in production control) for which engineers are used in the advanced countries.[18] For example, in the United States, firms use production engineers to reduce costs by increasing the efficiency of labor and other inputs. Under Brazilian conditions of relatively high costs for engineers and

17. The information that follows is based on interviews with company managers.

18. Eliminated some but not all: as noted in the next chapter, the sector's firms import much of their advanced technological knowledge through licensing agreements, but they still require engineering personnel both for internal development work and for adapting imported designs. As Table III-3 indicates, the Brazilian firms use almost as high a percentage of their engineers in research and development as do companies in the American machinery industry.

relatively low costs for other labor, however, firms have found it more economical to use fewer engineers and more labor. In effect, the Brazilian firms have substituted skilled and unskilled labor to save on the costs of engineers.

Secondly, for some of the technical jobs that remain, firms have lower hiring standards and use personnel without university education for positions which in the advanced countries are filled by graduate engineers. In this case, educational saving is similar to practices discussed earlier in connection with the lower formal-education attainment of Brazilian shop workers. A generation ago, some of the jobs in American industry presently held by graduate engineers were also filled by people without university education. With the rise of national income and expenditure on education, however, the supply of engineers relative to other labor grades has increased. Because of this shift in supply, firms hired graduate engineers for these functions, and the engineer coefficients have risen accordingly. By contrast, under Brazilian supply conditions, firms consider that for some jobs the relatively high costs of engineers are not justified by proportionate increases in productivity.[19]

These adjustments on the demand side have gone a considerable way toward meeting hypothetical "educational requirements," calculated by rigid application of the schooling coefficients of the work-force in the advanced countries. In the case of shop workers, economies of educational inputs save more than half of the formal education that would be required if the sector used American educational levels.[20] Part of these savings are probably costless, in the sense that more formal education would not increase worker productivity. This occurs in jobs whose performance requires no more formal education than the Brazilian workers have, along with innate intelligence and capacity for learning. In other cases, more schooling per worker and more use of engineers might raise

19. This flexibility in job-rating and employment practices has often given opportunity for upward mobility to people with less than professional formal education. These are the "self-made men" and "engineers without diplomas" often encountered in the sector—individuals who lacked the financial means to attend a university but attained their qualifications through experience and independent study.

20. That is, if the same unit of output requires 75 American workers with an average of twelve years of schooling per individual, the schooling stock is 900 educational years, in contrast to the 400 school years (100 workers with four years' schooling each) of the Brazilian workers.

productivity, but this would be offset by the higher cost of better educated personnel. Here educational saving is simply the response of firms to the relative factor-prices of their environment, and this adjustment is one of the conditions that enables the sector to compete with world market prices.[21]

THE SUPPLY OF EDUCATED AND SKILLED MANPOWER

IMPORTING HUMAN RESOURCES

In the sector's earliest period, trained manpower was supplied from the "seedbed" areas we have discussed: construction, the military, transportation, and other infrastructure activities. Immigrants from more advanced countries were also a major source of trained personnel. During the years 1924–1962, some two million people emigrated from Europe, Japan, and Mediterranean countries to Brazil.[22] Most of the immigrants were better educated, more skilled, and had more industrial experience than the average Brazilian worker who had been raised in São Paulo or in rural areas such as the Northeast. These newcomers raised the quality of the work-force in this sector and in other Brazilian industries. Immigrants have filled many jobs as foremen and skilled workers;[23] many of the engineers employed in this sector also were immigrants. This was especially true in earlier years, before the rapid growth of domestic engineer supply. Immigrant engineers and technicians played a crucial role in the domestic firms' transition from simple foundries and machine shops into full-fledged factories producing more complex products.

In addition to their immediate contribution to production, immigrants were important as technical instructors to Brazilians, for they had experience, on both the shop and management levels,

21. It might be thought that such educational saving is possible because of "lower level," or less capital-intensive, technology. In a study of the Dutch metalworking industry, however, G. K. Boon found that human capital inputs declined slightly, rather than increased, with higher levels of mechanization. See G. K. Boon, *Economic Choice of Human and Physical Factors in Production* (Amsterdam, 1964), pp. 253–254.

22. F. J. de Avila, "Brazil," in *The Economics of International Migration*, ed. Brinley Thomas (London, 1958), p. 186, Table 1, and *Anuário Estatístico*, various issues.

23. One detailed study of a metalworking firm of 400 employees, conducted in 1957, indicated that 95% of foremen and technicians and 62% of skilled workers and supervisors had been born outside Brazil. This is aside from the contribution made by the sons of immigrants. The percentages in this case may be overly high, but the case is probably not unusual. See J. R. B. Lopes, "O Ajustamento do Trabalhador à Indústria," in *Mobilidade Social e Trabalho*, ed. Bertram Hutchinson (Rio de Janeiro, 1958), p. 371, Table 1.

which was lacking in Brazil. The sector was thus supplied with a vital input, experience, which could be acquired only from previous production. By importing this factor, the sector was able to break out of the circle in which production of certain products was hampered by the lack of highly specific production experience.

Many of the immigrants were attracted to Brazil by the country's rapid economic growth and the expanding demand for labor skills.[24] Even though average per capita income was larger in the immigrants' countries of origin, wages for specific skills were often higher in Brazil. Moreover, the country's rapid economic development permitted faster upward mobility within the wage hierarchy than was usually possible in the immigrants' home countries. Immigration was also facilitated by Brazil's relatively free social structure. In the open society of São Paulo, immigrants did not face major institutional barriers to economic and social integration. The attractions were so great that European expatriates contracted for work in Brazil sometimes remained as immigrants.

Much has been said of the contribution that immigration can make to a country's economic development. At the least, because the cost of the immigrants' upbringing, education, and training has been borne by their country of origin, immigration may be a more economical way of acquiring specific skills than the alternatives: either investing resources to produce the skills domestically with local education and production experience, or importing them (paying transportation and incentive costs) in the form of foreign contract personnel.[25] Furthermore, as new and marginal members of society, immigrants may play a disproportionately large role in a traditional society as innovators and importers of novel practices. A large percentage of entrepreneurship in this sector and Brazilian industry as a whole has indeed been supplied by immigrants. Apart from these general considerations, however, we should note the very specific contributions that immigrants

24. Particularly in the postwar period, it is feasible to talk of skilled immigration being attracted by choice to Brazil, as opposed to the other countries open to large-scale immigration: Australia, Argentina, and other Latin American countries. Since Australia imposed limitations on immigration from Japan and the Mediterranean countries, the real choice for many would-be emigrants from those countries was between Brazil and other Latin American countries, such as Argentina, which have not offered such prospects of rapid economic growth during the postwar period.

25. Cf. G. O. Gutman, "Australian Economic Development," in *Public Policy: A Yearbook of the Graduate School of Public Administration, Harvard University*, vol. 9, ed. Carl J. Friedrich and Seymour E. Harris (Cambridge, Mass., 1959), pp. 244–246 and n. 9.

have made both by teaching the sector's domestic personnel and—through filling jobs in management, supervision, and production—in helping output to get under way and generate domestic sources of supply.

Almost all firms of the sector have also drawn upon the services of expatriates. In this case, because firms imported the specialized skills they required, the supply of skills was directly linked to the demands generated by investment and production plans. The domestic firms have imported engineers and technicians, both for production roles and to provide instruction to their own personnel in new product lines and techniques. Licensing and technical-assistance agreements with firms in the advanced countries have been especially useful for this purpose, for they have facilitated recruitment of manpower with the specific skills and production experience sought.

The foreign firms have also relied on expatriates. Upon establishing their Brazilian factories, they usually imported large numbers of contract personnel, generally from the company's home-country plants. Senior management (usually ranging down to department heads) and staff personnel were almost always imported; in some cases, foremen and master workmen were, too. The foreign firms have made much more lavish use of expatriates than have the domestic firms. One detailed study of personnel procedures of American firms in Brazil interprets this practice as a gross irrationality.[26] Companies often underestimated the capabilities of local personnel, and believed that establishment of a Brazilian subsidiary would be feasible only if they brought in many employees from their home plants. As a result, they often used expatriates who were perhaps four times as expensive as comparable domestic manpower.[27] These practices seem explicable, however, in terms of the firms' expectation that they would be able to exercise considerable market power in price determination, which would permit them to recoup their high personnel costs.

What is perhaps most notable about the use of expatriates in the sector, however, is the extent to which it has declined over time. The domestic firms now use foreign contract personnel only rarely, usually for very specific short-term consulting. The foreign firms

26. John C. Shearer, *High-Level Manpower in Overseas Subsidiaries* (Princeton, 1960), esp. pp. 124–132.
27. *Ibid.*, p. 117.

have also drastically reduced their use of expatriates. One firm, for example, which began with 40 expatriates, had by five years later replaced all but 10, and most of these were scheduled for substitution. Another much larger company originally had 300 contract personnel, but after five years only about 25 expatriates still remained. The experience of all other foreign firms in the sector has been similar.[28] The relatively few expatriates remaining have been in the highest administrative positions. Here the decisive criterion is generally the desire to maintain control of the firm by "company men" with many years of familiarity with and loyalty to the firm.[29]

Several factors have contributed to the reduction in the use of expatriates. First, competitive pressures within the sector forced firms to reconsider whether use of the expensive foreign personnel was really justified. This went along with a general upward revision in their evaluation of the capabilities of Brazilian managerial and technical personnel.[30] Secondly, for jobs where specific technical knowledge and production experience had previously been lacking, local production—begun with the help of imported personnel—

28. In some cases, firms still give an impression of overwhelming predominance of foreign personnel, especially at their head offices. This is somewhat misleading, for many of the personnel observed (e.g., secretaries) are not expatriates but immigrants or the offspring of immigrants to Brazil from the various European countries where the firm's home offices are. Because of their knowledge of the firm's home-country language, they can usually earn more there than elsewhere. Such personnel add greatly to the "German" or "French" atmosphere of the companies where they are employed, and give a misleading impression of the extent of skill importation.

29. The hiring criterion here is not only political—i.e., loyalty to the foreign company in case of a conflict with the interests of the host country. Perhaps even more important is long experience with the mores of the complex social institution constituted by "The Company." In many cases, nationals of the same foreign country would also be ineligible, for they too would not have had the years of socialization necessary for high leadership positions within these institutions. By this criterion, a Brazilian who has spent years within the corporation and could be considered a "company man" is a much more likely candidate for top management positions than a person of the same national origin as the company but brought in "from outside."

30. The sector's experience in this respect contrasts with what is recounted by Shearer (*High-Level Manpower*, pp. 115–132). Shearer's 1958 field research indicated that for internal reasons, American firms in Brazil (and Mexico) had not gone very far in replacing expatriates with qualified domestic personnel. Despite the much higher salary costs of expatriates, widespread use of contract personnel continued even for jobs where capable domestic personnel were available. My own observations in some foreign firms, both American and European, in other Brazilian industries during 1964 also indicated a much greater prevalence of foreign personnel than was common in the capital goods sector. The major factor explaining these differences seems to be the fierce competition in the heavy-engineering products sector. For lack of market power, the foreign firms here cannot set wages at discretion and pay the higher salaries required for expatriates.

increased the domestic supply of specialized skills and experience. With greater availability of qualified Brazilians, the more expensive expatriates could no longer compete in the labor market.[31]

The sector's experience with immigrants and expatriates shows how importation of trained personnel can be used to deal with deficiencies in domestic educational and skill resources. Another feature of the sector's experience has been that the higher output associated with use of imported manpower has usually increased rather than reduced demand for skills supplied domestically. For example, as firms employed foreign engineers for jobs in which experience was not yet available in Brazil, they also hired Brazilian engineers to fill other jobs that had been created. Domestic and foreign personnel with different capabilities have been complementary rather than competitive resources, and as output rose with the aid of imported skills, the demand for domestic personnel at all levels increased, too.

THE SUPPLY OF ENGINEERS

In the past generation, the supply of engineers in Brazil has increased rapidly. Table III–4 presents data on the growth of

TABLE III-4. Enrollment in Brazilian Engineering Schools, 1938–1961

Year	Number of students	Index
1938	2,010	100
1943	3,070	153
1948	5,870	293
1953	7,050	352
1961	13,380	678

Sources: Calculated from A. F. Faust, *Brazil: Education in an Expanding Economy* (Washington, D.C., 1963), Table 20; and Ministério da Educação, *Sinopse Estatística do Ensino Superior* (Rio de Janeiro, 1963).

enrollments in Brazilian engineering schools between 1938 and 1961. Engineering enrollments grew at an annual cumulative rate of 8.7 percent, with an equally high rate of growth in the number of

31. Pressures from the Brazilian government to reduce use of imported personnel do not seem to have been an important force, as compared with the economic pressures cited. Cf. Shearer, *High-Level Manpower*, pp. 122–127.

TABLE III-5. Cumulative Annual Growth Rates of Engineering-student Enrollment in Brazil (1938–1961) and Selected Other Countries (1950–1959)

Country	Cumulative annual growth rate (Percent)	Number of students in base year	Number of students at end of period
Brazil, 1938–1961	8.7	2,010	13,380
Belgium	4.9	2,260	3,460
Canada	6.2	9,020	15,540
Denmark	2.8	2,240	2,850
France	6.0	8,900	15,000
West Germany	6.3	18,010	31,100
Greece	5.0	1,100	1,700
Italy	3.0	16,400	21,580
Netherlands	2.8	5,620	7,190
Norway	6.4	1,050	1,830
Spain	7.3	2,720	4,770
Sweden	5.9	2,870	4,770
Switzerland	3.8	1,890	2,270
Turkey	12.1	2,513	5,600
United Kingdom (1950–58)	6.2	10,600	16,910
United States	4.8	180,260	278,350
Yugoslavia	12.1	8,530	19,620

Source: Calculated from OECD, *Resources of Scientific and Technical Personnel in the OECD Area* (Paris, 1964), Appendix, Table 5. The choice of periods for countries other than Brazil was dictated by the data available in this publication.

engineers graduated.[32] This increase exceeded the high rates of Brazilian aggregate growth, though it was slightly below the pace of industrial expansion. Table III–5 compares the growth of engineering enrollments in Brazil with the experience of other countries. As we see, the Brazilian rate of expansion has been high compared to most of the other countries. This record is all the more impressive because these growth rates were maintained over a relatively long period, more than double that cited for the other countries.

Not only has the supply of engineers increased rapidly, but their distribution among various specialties also changed radically during

32. Calculated from statistics supplied by the Ministry of Education and published in Harold R. W. Benjamin, *Higher Education in the American Republics* (New York, 1965), p. 153, Table 21.

this period. In contrast with the previous emphasis on civil engine-ering and architecture, a much larger percentage of students came to specialize in the newer fields such as mechanical and electrical

TABLE III-6. Students' Specialization in São Paulo State Engineering Schools, 1954 and 1962 (Percent)

Specialization	1954	1962
Mechanical, electrical, metallurgical, chemical, and industrial engineering	27	47
Civil engineering, architecture	71	38
Other	2	15
	100	100

Source: Calculated from Govêrno Adhemar de Barros, *Plano de Desenvolvimento Integrado* (São Paulo, 1964), pp. 110–111.

engineering. Table III–6 shows the extent of the change in student specialization in the engineering schools of São Paulo State during the recent period. The percentage of students specializing in the newer fields almost doubled in the eight years between 1954 and 1962. As a result, the number of engineers with the skills required by the capital goods industry and Brazil's other new industries rose rapidly, both because of the large increases in overall engine-ering enrollments and because of the changed distribution of specialization within these larger numbers of engineers.

Social conditions associated with the increased supply of engineers. What were some of the social and economic conditions that appear to have been responsible for this increased supply of engineers? First of all, Brazilian society accords considerable prestige to higher education.[33] This valuation is associated with the tradition of *doutorismo:* the close connection that has traditionally linked high status and higher education. Demands for education have also increased as a result of the extensive changes that have affected the old order in Brazil, particularly since 1929. These were evident politically in the Vargas Revolution of 1930; and in the economic sphere, with the 1929 coffee debacle and the subsequent accelera-tion of industrialization.

33. Cf., e.g., the survey data gathered in Kalman H. Silvert and Frank Bonilla, *Education and the Social Meaning of Development: A Preliminary Statement* (New York, 1961).

These changes had an important impact on the demand for education. With rapid economic development, the number of middle- and upper-class positions increased. Entrance into these positions usually required higher educational qualifications. At the same time, educational expenditures were facilitated by the higher income levels concurrent with economic growth. Furthermore, economic development was accompanied by social restratification. São Paulo has had a very high degree of social mobility, both upward *and* downward.[34] These social changes made it more feasible to think of expenditure on higher educational qualifications as an investment. For, with the loosening of the traditional hierarchy, middle-strata Brazilians of domestic or immigrant origins could realistically aspire to greater upward mobility. Increased freedom in the labor market and the spread of universalistic employment criteria also meant that institutional barriers were less likely to prevent entrance into higher positions and keep individuals from enjoying the fruits of investment in greater educational attainments. Furthermore, in an effort to maintain their upper-class positions in a new and more competitive society, members of the traditional elite also increased their demands for higher education.

Along with the growing importance accorded education in general has gone a greater interest in higher technical education, caused by a significant shift in educational values since the 1930's. As was the case in many other Latin American countries, Brazilian higher education had traditionally stressed literary and legal studies oriented to the interests of a leisure class or a career in law or the civil service. As the traditional elite was successfully challenged in the political and economic spheres, the older educational values also lost their authority.[35] Particularly in São Paulo, new emphasis was placed on "technical" and "pragmatic" studies, in conscious contrast to the former "humanistic" tradition.

34. See the international comparisons presented in S. M. Lipset and R. Bendix, *Social Mobility in Industrial Society* (Berkeley, 1959), pp. 27–31. Data on mobility in São Paulo were gathered in Bertram Hutchinson's pioneering study of the late 1950's, *Mobilidade Social e Trabalho.*

35. There is some reference to this movement, particularly the work of reformers such as Anísio Teixeira and Fernando de Azevedo in reshaping the primary school system, in Havighurst and Moreira, *Society and Education in Brazil,* pp. 91–92. A complete history of the rethinking of the country's intellectual tradition and reshaping of higher educational institutions that went on during this period is not yet available.

The growing success and achievements of Brazilian industrialization supported these ideas. What had formerly been the ideas of a small group of deviants now acquired respectability for wider segments of the public. As industrial expansion proceeded and the demands for engineers multiplied, it became realistic to see a future in a technical education. Individuals trying to orient themselves in rapidly changing social and economic conditions often considered industrialization synonymous with more opportunities for engineers, and they made their educational and career plans accordingly.

Increased interest in higher technical education has affected both the demand for and the supply of facilities for education of engineers. On the demand side, would-be students and their parents have put pressure on the existing schools to expand. On the supply side, university administrators and politicians involved in educational allocations have been relatively sensitive to the need for rapid expansion of the engineering schools. For example, in 1962 a new engineering school was founded in São Paulo, pending certification by the federal authorities. Under the impetus of an intensive political campaign, including letter-writing and lobbying by students and their parents, official certification was granted within the relatively short period of several weeks. As a result of this pressure of demand and responsiveness of supply, engineering enrollments were able to expand rapidly enough to permit the sustained, high growth rates noted earlier.

Engineering school facilities in São Paulo have grown both through the expansion of the older institutions and through the founding of four new schools, under private, clerical, military, and regional auspices. These new institutions tapped sources of financial and political support that were not available to the existing schools. Establishment of the new schools was also possible because, in contrast with the pattern in some other Latin American countries, the older institutions did not attempt to maintain a monopoly position, but adopted a "freedom of entry" policy toward new schools. This attitude was probably related to the enormous pressure on existing facilities and to the general expansionary climate surrounding Brazilian education.

The social conditions that we have discussed, particularly social restratification and a shift in educational values, have been essential to the continued rapid rise in the supply of engineering graduates. These factors have been strongly reinforced by the economic conditions affecting the supply of engineers in Brazil.

Economic conditions associated with increased supply of engineers. Table III–7 presents data on the relative wages of unskilled industrial workers and graduate engineers with several years of experience in the sector. These figures are compared with the relative wage for equivalent manpower grades in the same sector of several advanced countries. The data indicate a wage structure in which the relative wage of the Brazilian engineers is approximately two and one-half times higher than in the advanced countries.[36]

TABLE III-7. Salary of Experienced Engineers Relative to Wage of Unskilled Workers in the Capital Goods Industry of Brazil and of Advanced Countries

Country	Ratio of engineers' salary to minimum industrial wage
Brazil	12.0
West Germany	4.0
Japan	5.0
United Kingdom	4.5
United States	5.5

Source: Data supplied by officials of the foreign firms in the sector on wages paid to personnel in the same function in their Brazilian and in their home-country plants.

Unlike the situation in some less-developed countries, this high differential does not appear to be caused by institutional conditions, such as a predatory upper class, social convention, or use of foreign salary scales (for example, by international oil companies), which

36. It might be thought that the high Brazilian differential is based essentially on the low wages of industrial workers transferred from the rural sector at a low opportunity cost reflecting low agricultural productivity and wages. (Cf. W. A. Lewis, "Economic Development with Unlimited Supplies of Labor," reprinted in *The Economics of Underdevelopment*, ed. Agarwala and Singh, esp. pp. 409–411). Minimum industrial wages in Brazil, however, are at least twice the level of agricultural wages. (See W. M. Nicholls and R. M. Paiva, "Structure and Productivity of Brazilian Agriculture," mimeographed [Vanderbilt University, 1964], pp. 9, 51, 53.)

determine wage rates far above a competitive-market equilibrium. Nor is Brazil like some post-colonial African countries where the indigenous civil servants impose salaries at the level of the former expatriates, salaries that are considerably higher than the domestic supply prices. In such circumstances, with an institutionally determined wage above market-equilibrium levels, we would expect substantial unemployment of these labor grades; and in fact, this is often reported in such situations. In Brazil, however, there has been no unemployment of engineers. This suggests that their marginal value product still exceeds their wages, and that the high wage differential results from factors other than institutional distortions. The high Brazilian relative wage seems to be caused by the fact that although supply of engineers has increased very rapidly, demand has risen at least as fast. With high rates of growth in the demand for manufactured products, demand for engineers has risen so much that the large increases in supply have not prevented a situation of scarcity (reflected in their high relative wage) for engineers.[37]

The supply of engineers has not kept pace with the demands of the labor market principally because of the insufficient expansion of the educational system. The number of places for engineering students did increase enough to permit an 8.7-percent compound growth rate. But student demands for engineering education have grown even faster, and would have permitted still larger increases in the number of engineers graduated, had more places been available. In recent years, the São Paulo engineering schools have admitted their full complement of students, but have had to exclude some five to eight applicants for every available place.[38] Because of this insufficient expansion of facilities, excess demand for engineering education has developed, which has been contained only by quantity rationing. This has been done by the imposition of queuing, and by raising admission standards. If the schools had grown more rapidly, however, these expedients would not have had to be adopted, and enrollments would have been more ade-

37. Fragmentary evidence from firms in the sector with salary data going back to the early 1950's indicates no upward or downward trend in the relative wage of engineers in the course of the past decade.
38. Evidence is from deans of the São Paulo universities. Except for the medical schools, the number of excess applicants for available places was generally lower in the other university faculties than for engineering studies.

quate to the demands of the labor market.[39] Because of the barrier to entry into the profession posed by the constraint of the educational system's limited expansion, the engineers who do graduate receive a quasi-rent reflecting their scarcity value and raising their salaries.

This relatively high salary has provided a substantial incentive for individuals to acquire an engineering education. The private costs of acquiring such training, including tuition and foregone earnings, are relatively low compared with the returns made possible by higher future income. Under recent Brazilian conditions, the private benefit-cost ratio of an engineering education, computed with a 10-percent discount rate, is approximately 4.0.[40] The gains of engineering education are large precisely because of the high relative wage, which means that the opportunity costs of staying out of the work-force are low relative to the higher income stream made possible by an engineering education. Because of this

39. It is not easy to say that the engineering schools *could* have been expanded much more rapidly over long periods of time. On the basis of extensive experience in education planning in less-developed countries, Russell Davis of the Harvard Center for Studies in Education and Development has, in oral communication, mentioned 8–10% per annum as an upper bound for sustained expansion of an educational system as a whole. This technical and administrative limit was probably approached; for all of Brazilian higher education was expanding at comparably high rates during this period. (See the data in A. F. Faust, *Brazil: Education in an Expanding Economy* [Washington, D.C., 1963], table 20). Benefit/cost analysis of the different sectors of Brazilian higher education, however, might have indicated that it would have been worthwhile to expand engineering education more rapidly, at the expense of less rapid growth elsewhere.

40. This calculation has been arrived at by taking the discounted value of the earnings stream of a secondary-school graduate 21 years old who enters the São Paulo labor force, and comparing it with the discounted future income of the graduate who enters engineering school for the Brazilian five-year study period. The calculation, B/Q is based on the formula

$$B = \sum_{\tau=6}^{L} \frac{(Y\tau - Y'\tau)}{(1+i)^{\tau+1}},$$

$$Q = \sum_{\tau=1}^{5} \frac{(C\tau + Y'\tau)}{(1+i)^{\tau+1}}$$

Date on Y and Y', the earnings and the earnings foregone of engineers, are from personnel directors of industrial firms in São Paulo. Data on tuition costs, C are from São Paulo engineering schools. Data on length of lifetime, L are from the United Nations' *Demographic Yearbook, 1963* (New York, 1964), p. 618. The discount rate, i, is 10%. The present value of the private benefits from engineering education is 22,995 *contos* (mid-1964 *conto*), and the discounted private costs are 5,574 *contos*, giving a ratio B/Q of 3.996. The break-even point, at which discounted value of gains equals discounted value of costs, is reached at age 32. The benefit/cost ratio would be considerably larger, and the payoff period considerably shorter, of course, in cases where a discount rate lower than 10% is used, e.g., when, for lack of a family business or investment opportunities available from a well-organized capital market, profitable alternative uses for savings are not available. In such instances, particularly under Brazil's continual inflation, individuals may well apply a lower discount rate.

incentive, although inadequate educational facilities prevented the engineer supply from increasing fast enough to do away with the scarcity rent, the supply response was sufficient to permit the dynamic growth that has been observed.

Similar market forces also seem to have been instrumental in changing the sectoral distribution of engineer supply noted in Table III–6. With the development of industries generating demand for mechanical and electrical engineers, their salaries increased more rapidly than those in the older fields. At the level of recently graduated engineers, a wage differential of approximately 50 percent emerged in favor of the new specialties.[41] Here too, supply seems to have adjusted to changes in demand, which made themselves felt through movements of relative prices.

TRAINING PROGRAMS FOR ENGINEERS

The schooling of engineers is only a step in fulfilling the sector's demands for engineers. Newly educated engineering graduates are the raw material from which personnel with specialized skills and experience are fashioned. Programs maintained by firms of the sector have been an important source of such training.

Almost all firms in the sector maintain training programs for their engineers. These usually emphasize specialized technical knowledge in fabrication of the firm's specific products. The foreign firms send Brazilian personnel for periods ranging from a few months to more than a year to plants located in their home countries, in order to learn company policies and production techniques. The larger domestic firms also send personnel abroad for training and study. Licensing agreements with companies in the advanced countries have been of crucial importance in enabling the domestic firms to place personnel with overseas companies in the specific trades they were seeking. Firms have also supported training courses within the company or at local universities. For example, a professional engineers' society, the Associação Brasileira de Metais, has organized well-attended, specialized instruction programs which have been supported by industrial firms. The National Steel Company, whose mechanical subsidiary is one of the firms in the heavy-engineering sector, has the most extensive

41. The personnel directors of firms of the sector supplied this information. An even larger differential appeared for more experienced personnel.

training program. Located far from other educational facilities, it has established a system of company schools whose curricula range from basic literacy courses for bench workers to a full-fledged engineering program for management and technical personnel. Finally, firms have also provided paid traineeships for engineering students. During these traineeships and other apprenticeship programs for newly recruited engineers, firms have generally overcome the students' prejudice against work involving "dirty hands." Companies have made a direct attack on this attitude, for they consider it a serious obstacle to full utilization of an engineer's capabilities. The process of learning this new behavior has been facilitated by the social context of the apprenticeship, for the young engineer's professional superiors usually provide an example. Direct incentives for learning are also present, since promotion or dismissal by the firm usually depends on it. Annual expenditure by the firms on their training programs, both for management and for foremen and shop personnel, amounts to approximately 0.5 percent of gross sales.[42] In cases of firms preparing personnel for large new operations, costs are usually higher.

Because of the importance of these programs in the supply of specialized training, it is important to understand why firms make such efforts. The question is particularly interesting because they may have no assurance that they will themselves appropriate the gains from these investments. After having undergone training, personnel may move to another firm, quite possibly to a competitor. Hence training programs may only weaken a firm's market position. To pose the question more acutely: the competing firm may pay higher salaries precisely because it does not have the expense of training efforts. Alternatively, even if the worker does remain with the company which trained him, he may do so only for a higher wage that fully reflects his increased productivity— that is, at the wage determined by what he could obtain with his new skills anywhere else in the labor market.

Nevertheless, firms have found it worthwhile to maintain training programs. Investment in training has yielded high returns because of the sharply increased productivity of personnel with needed skills. This reflects demand conditions, the value of complementary

42. Computed from information supplied by firms in the sector.

resources, and the limited elasticity of substitution between some skills and other inputs in the sector's production technology. At the same time, firms have been able to appropriate for themselves enough of the net benefit to provide a reasonable return from their training activities.[43]

First, labor-market imperfections have limited the mobility of trainees, and reduced the probability of their leaving the firm or claiming the full measure of their increased productivity in higher wages.[44] Especially for the more costly programs, firms usually train personnel only after a selection process by which they exclude people who they consider will be likely to leave the firm afterward. The more expensive programs are generally restricted to personnel who have been with the firm for several years. In these cases, the personal and social ties integrating individuals within the firm reduce mobility and increase the size of the salary differential needed to induce these people to move to other companies.[45] Furthermore, because of accumulated seniority, such long-term employees may also have a salary advantage in remaining with their present firm. In addition, their experience may give them a special familiarity with the company's production equipment and product line, and thus higher productivity and wages than they could get elsewhere. These advantages of remaining with a particular firm could not be matched by moving elsewhere.

Barriers to labor mobility have also been reinforced by "gentlemen's agreements" among firms attempting to reduce the extent of pirating. Apart from the "ethical" consideration involved, these agreements have been given force by the fear of retaliation and of the general salary rise that might follow upon large-scale raiding campaigns. Such agreements have not had total compliance, and for pressing individual needs all firms have resorted to raiding. In particular, firms in distant labor markets and new firms anxious

43. The discussion in the next paragraphs follows the general lines of Gary Becker's theoretical formulation, in "Investment in Human Capital." In this case, however, the departures from the competitive market model prove to be the essence of the story.

44. Even though, for the reasons discussed below, companies can appropriate a good part of the gains from training, the increased productivity resulting from provision of specialized training has been so high that trainees have usually been paid salaries that are above levels of un-trained personnel both during and after the training period.

45. These factors help explain why most training is done by paternalistic companies. These may be either "old-fashioned," family-type firms or self-consciously "modern" corporations with a "social policy" integrating workers to the firm. In either case, the personal and social ties linking employees to the company are generally strong.

to start production have been noted for extensive pirating campaigns; in both cases, the pressures for trained personnel outweighed costs of retaliation. Such individual pirating, however, has not reduced the firms' gains to a point so low that discontinuance of training was warranted.

Although some individuals may be pirated, firms are concerned with the overall probability of retaining enough trainees—not necessarily all—to make their programs worthwhile. Increased productivity through training may be so high that returns to the firm are sufficient even with a high loss rate. That is, firms will continue training as long as:

$$\frac{G}{K} \cdot P > R,$$

where G is the (time-discounted) rise in the productivity of trained personnel; K is the cost of training; P the probability of retaining trainees within the firm; and R the cost of capital to the firm.

For the sector's firms, this condition seems to have been met. The values of G have often been so high relative to K that they have persisted in training efforts despite subsequent losses of trainees to other, often competing, companies. Although the measures cited earlier probably reduce mobility, losses of 25 percent of trainees immediately upon termination of training programs are common in the sector. Another study cites even higher immediate losses, reaching 40 percent.[46] Firms may resent such losses bitterly, or they may recognize them as part of the normal factor mobility from which they themselves have also benefited. In either case, although pirating is a very annoying problem for management, prompting frequent review of the advisability of their training programs, losses are accepted as a matter of course, and training programs are continued. (Indeed, as long as the condition formulated above is satisfied, the rational response of a firm losing part of its trainees is to *expand* its training program in order to increase the number retained.)

Training has also been worthwhile for individual firms because of the oligopsonistic labor market conditions which prevail for the purchase of highly specialized skills.[47] As suggested by the pre-

46. Shearer, *High-Level Manpower*, pp. 110–111, 124–132.
47. Becker, "Investment in Human Capital," pp. 24–25, also stresses the importance of power in the factor market in making training worthwhile for individual firms.

viously cited management fear of raising salaries through pirating, we cannot always assume a competitive market-equilibrium with factors receiving their full marginal-value products. In cases when firms are one of the few buyers of specialized skills—for example, engineering expertise in paper-making or petrochemical equipment—they exercise considerable market power in determining wages. In these cases, scarcity conditions may create so large a potential quasi-rent that even when a firm pays wages. that are high by conventional Brazilian standards, it can pay sufficiently less than full marginal product to appropriate much of the gains from training.[48]

Furthermore, apart from power to administer wages, firms perceiving an upward-sloping supply curve for specific manpower grades may attempt to lower their wage costs by adding to supply through training. By increasing the aggregate supply of these specialized skills, they then pay a lower wage than would otherwise have prevailed. Such training is not necessarily stopped if firms subsequently lose personnel whom they have trained, or if after the traineeship wages rise to reflect higher productivity. Although the firm may lose specific individuals through pirating, the wages it must pay for replacements are also lower because of the increase in supply and the consequent lower market wage.

In particular, large, new firms have felt that because of the effects of their demands on marginal wage rates, "it was cheaper to train than to pirate." When the foreign firms entered the sector, for example, the impact of their large and discontinuous demand on existing skill supply was so great that wage rates rose very sharply. Firms which located their plants in areas far from the large labor pools encountered these problems in especially acute form. Relatively high wages have been necessary to attract skilled workers to such new areas: first, because geographical distance reduced labor mobility; second, because housing supply was inelastic, so that the salaries needed to attract new personnel had to compensate for sharply rising residential rents.

Firms' decisions to provide training have, of course, been

48. Although certain highly specific skills purchased under oligopsonistic conditions may not receive their full marginal value product, they are still well enough rewarded, as we have seen, to provide an ample inducement to the employee to acquire training. The inadequacies of supply cannot be attributed to any dampening of incentives by oligopsonistic factor markets.

heavily influenced by conditions in their product market. And training has usually been a less expensive way of acquiring skills than the alternative of importation. In cases where, for technological reasons, lack of specific skills constituted a bottleneck to production and sales in a potentially profitable market, even high salaries paid to trainees have been below the (indeterminate) marginal value product, and firms have felt no hesitation about training.

THE SUPPLY OF SKILLED WORKERS

Table III–8 indicates the supply of people with primary education—the basic educational input for the skilled labor force in the sector. Enrollments grew at an annual cumulative growth rate of 4.2 percent over 28 years, a rate exceeding the growth of population and providing a labor force of increasing basic educational attainment.[49] The supply of skilled workers (*qualificados*) in the sector and in the capital goods industry in general increased at an even faster rate. In the period 1951–1963, the number of skilled workers in the metalworking industries of São Paulo State rose from approximately 24,700 to 75,000, at an annual cumulative rate of 10.4 percent.[50]

TABLE III-8. Increase in Primary School Enrollments in Brazil, 1933–1961

Year	Number of Students	Index
1933	2,108,000	100
1938	2,902,000	137
1943	3,075,000	146
1948	3,913,000	158
1953	4,827,000	228
1961	6,711,000	318

Sources: Brazilian *Anuário Estatístico*, various issues; and A. F. Faust, *Brazil: Education in an Expanding Economy* (Washington, D.C., 1963), p. 46, Table 5.

49. Primary-school enrollments increased only half as rapidly as the engineering-school enrollments noted in Table III-4. Data in the *Anuário Estatístico* and in Havighurst and Moleira, *Society and Education in Brazil*, indicate that secondary education has also expanded at much higher rates than primary education during the past generation. The reasons for the varying rates of expansion on the different educational levels are not clear. They may have been conditioned by the changed pattern of demands coming with economic development; by conditions on the supply side related to the distribution of income; and by factors internal to the educational system itself.

50. Calculated from data in *SENAI: Relatório de 1963*, (São Paulo, 1964), pp. 4–10.

Despite these large increases in supply, scarcity conditions in the market for skilled workers have prevailed, as reflected in a high relative wage for such workers. Data on the relative wage of master workmen in the capital goods industry of Brazil and of several advanced countries are presented in Table III–9. The relative

TABLE III-9. Wages of Master Workmen Relative to Those of Unskilled Workers in the Capital Goods Industry of Brazil and of Advanced Countries

Country	Ratio of master workmen's wage to minimum industrial wage
Brazil	4.2
West Germany	2.5
Japan	2.5
United Kingdom	2.2
United States	3.2

Source: Data supplied by the executives of the foreign firms in the sector.

wages of skilled workers in the Brazilian sector are between 30 and 90 percent higher than in the advanced countries.[51] Seen in historical terms, the Brazilian relative wage is also high: more than double that of skilled personnel in the metalworking trades in the United States during the period 1860–1890.[52]

As in the case of engineers, the high wage differential for skilled workers seems to reflect the failure of skill supply to keep pace with

51. As compared with the other advanced industrial countries, the relative wage of highly skilled workers in the United States is also fairly high. Lloyd Reynolds has explained this wage structure in terms of labor-market imperfections and administered wage-setting by management rather than seeing it as an incentive necessary to generate supply of skilled workers. See his *The Structure of Labor Markets* (New York, 1951), pp. 238–240.

52. Cf. R. Ozanne, "A Century of Occupational Differentials in Manufacturing," *Review of Economics and Statistics*, 44 (August 1962), esp. the data in Table II, p. 293. The low American wage differential in the nineteenth century is usually explained in terms of: (1) relatively high level of minimum industrial wages because of abundance of fertile lands in the West; (2) the importance of immigration as a supply of skilled workers; and (3) the relatively slow pace of industrialization which limited movements of the demand curve for skilled workers. As suggested below, the principal difference between American and Brazilian wage differentials seems to be this last factor: the more rapid pace of Brazilian industrialization has meant sharply expanding demand for skilled personnel.

rapidly growing demands. With the rapid expansion of the Brazilian metalworking industries, demands for skilled personnel have risen sharply. Despite a significant increase, the supply of skilled workers has not risen sufficiently to prevent the wages of skilled personnel from being bid up, giving rise to scarcity rents and the high relative wage.[53]

Scarcity of engineers appeared to be caused by the inadequate expansion of the educational system. Because of the large number of upper- and middle-income families able to bear the costs of an engineering education and the high returns to such an investment, there has even been excess demand for places in the engineering schools. Scarcity of highly skilled workers, however, appears to have a different cause, namely, insufficient effective demand for training in higher skills. This, in turn, results from low income and savings levels, and the unavailability of lending facilities that would permit workers to finance investment in higher qualifications.

Because of the high relative wage, the net gain of acquiring higher skills for shop personnel is extremely large. For example, the private benefit/cost ratio, calculated with a 10 percent discount rate, of moving from the intermediate skill level of a machinist to the higher level of a toolmaker is approximately 16.7.[54] Because of the difficulty of financing such training, however, relatively few workers have been able to respond effectively to this incentive.[55] Hence the high relative wage seems to be a comment on the relative absence of subsidized training facilities as well as a reflection of

53. The high Brazilian relative wage does not stem from labor-market imperfections introduced by strong craft unions. The sector's unions are organized on an industrial rather than a craft basis, and there has been a notably open attitude toward entry into skilled positions.

54. Before training, a machinist would be receiving approximately 75 *contos* (mid-1964) per month; after training, 100 *contos*. (Data are from personnel directors of firms in the sector.) Provision of training in an intensive program would cost approximately 207 *contos*, of which 150 would be for his foregone earnings during the 2-month training period, and 57 *contos* for cost of equipment and personnel used in instruction. (Data on training times and costs are from *Ensino Industrial*, 3, no. 7 [1964], p. 4, Tables I-2, and are based on a training project conducted by the Industrial Training Division of the Brazilian Ministry of Education in 1964.) If the future lifetime of a 25-year-old Brazilian worker is 35 years (cf. data from the *Demographic Yearbook*), applying a discount rate of 10% to the additional annual income of 360 *contos* gives a ratio $B/Q = 16.7$.

55. This difference from the situation underlying the high relative wage differentials for engineers conforms to Becker's suggestion ("Investment in Human Capital," p. 42) that because of capital-market deficiencies for financing human capital investments, internal financing would be common, and wealthier families would be better able to make such investments.

capital-market conditions that prevent workers from borrowing to finance the acquisition of higher skills.[56]

Despite these difficulties, the return on investment in training has provided an inducement to some workers to save enough from current income to finance their training. To service this demand, in São Paulo, approximately 40 private night schools with places for 2000 students have emerged, staffed by master workmen and engineers supplementing their income by evening teaching.[57] Design reading, a prerequisite for skilled-worker and foreman positions, has been the major curriculum item of these schools. Tuition charges have been from 8 to 20 percent of the income of workers studying in these night courses. They have also required a commitment of several hours a week—in addition to a 55-hour work week—for periods ranging from six months to three years. When questioned about their reasons for making such sacrifices, participants invariably reply in terms of a private investment calculation, usually expressed in terms of the large wage differential, and the short pay-out period necessary to recover their investment in training.[58]

TRAINING PROGRAMS FOR SHOP WORKERS

Firms in the sector also have maintained training programs for their shop workers, albeit on a much smaller scale than for their engineers and management personnel.[59] Returns to the firm are apparently higher from training expenditure in highly specific engineering skills, otherwise not available, especially because they have much greater market power in determining salaries for such manpower.

Programs for shop workers have usually focused on the training

56. Capital-market imperfections seem to be the main factor at work here, rather than the high transactions costs that would be involved in administering a program of very small individual loans for training purposes. Small loans have been provided commercially for financing installment buying of consumer purchases of small unit price despite the large percentage weight of transaction costs. The main difference in the credit situation for financing training appears to be the lack of availability of physical assets for repossession in case of default.

57. Data are from personnel directors and training personnel in São Paulo.

58. Information comes from interviews with foremen and master workers in factories of the sector.

59. This pattern of higher training allocations for management personnel is similar to what was observed in the United States by J. Mincer, in "On-the-job Training: Costs, Returns, and Some Implications," *Journal of Political Economy*, 70, pt. 2 (October 1962) 59.

of foremen and supervisors, with trainees recruited from the plant's senior workers. In some cases firms have paid at least part of the tuition of workers attending private training schools. In others, they have initiated programs within the firm, either during or after working hours. The principal subjects taught are design reading and machinery use, and sometimes arithmetic and Portuguese, to permit further technical learning. Courses for foremen have sometimes included instruction in "human relations," to facilitate managing of work groups. The foreign firms often provide instruction in the language of the company's country of origin, as an aid for communication with higher management personnel.

Company training for shop personnel has concentrated on foremen because this has been the grade of shop labor for which firms have encountered the least elastic supply. Barriers to mobility such as personal ties to the firm, accumulated seniority, and the specific advantages of remaining with a particular firm have likewise been most important for the long-time workers usually selected as foremen.

Firms have also provided some training for skilled workers. This has usually been in skills specific to their own production equipment or product line. In such cases, the increased productivity of trained personnel, and the firm's market power in the purchase of these highly specialized skills, has made training profitable for companies even when paying their trainees wages which are relatively high by Brazilian standards. Firms located far from the large labor pools have also provided extensive training for large numbers of unskilled and semiskilled workers. Here it has been worthwhile to increase the local supply of trained workers both because of geographic immobility and the inelasticity of supply of skilled personnel to—and subsequently from—these areas, and because of the firms' oligopsonistic power in local labor markets. Some large new firms began training while the company's factory was being built, so that a qualified labor force would be ready upon its completion. In these programs, firms have paid their trainees at the minimum industrial wage for periods longer than a year. Master workmen and company engineers have served as instructors.

Because of the high relative wage for skilled workers, the number of applicants for training programs has greatly exceeded the number that firms have wanted to train, so that they have been able to choose from among the individuals whose productivity is likely to increase most from training. As standard practice within the sector, applicants for training have undergone screening tests in arithmetic and literacy, intelligence, and mechanical aptitude.

THE SENAI

Another training program has been maintained under legal compulsion, through a unique, semi-official institution, the SENAI (Serviço Nacional de Aprendizagem Industrial; National Industrial Apprenticeship Service). The SENAI was founded under the leadership of Roberto Simonsen of the São Paulo Federation of Industries at the outset of World War II. To increase the domestic supply of skilled workers and cope with the shortages which resulted from the cessation of immigration of trained manpower from Europe, the government levied a 1-percent payroll tax, the receipts of which were earmarked for industrial training, under the jurisdiction of the Federation and the government. Using training practices and personnel first developed in the railroads, programs were initiated which soon came under the direction of professional training specialists.

The SENAI has provided both apprenticeships for young workers and adult industrial education. Under the apprenticeship program, fourteen-year-old boys apply to individual firms for training. The boys selected undergo an apprentice period of three years, during which they are paid the minimum industrial wage. Their time is allocated half to "theory"—arithmetic, design reading, and machinery instruction, and half to "practice"— in-plant training at the workbench. Instruction may take place either within the firm or at SENAI schools.

In its training for adult workers, the SENAI has provided regular day and night courses for foremen and skilled workers, as well as special programs for needs which the SENAI's manpower surveys indicate are in especially short supply. In 1963 the SENAI of São Paulo maintained 38 schools, with 461 different courses and a total enrollment of 17,720, approximately 1.5 percent of the industrial work force.[60] These programs constitute the most important source of formally organized, general industrial training.

60. *SENAI Relatório*, p. 2.

Between its inception in 1943 and 1961, the SENAI contributed to the training of approximately 57 percent of the increment of skilled workers in all trades of the São Paulo State industrial work force.[61] In the heavy-engineering sector, approximately 30 percent of the skilled workers have had SENAI training.[62]

Because of the absence of other subsidized sources of training, the SENAI's relatively large percentage contribution to the supply of skilled labor is not surprising. Despite dedicated and imaginative efforts, however, the SENAI training program has not been sufficient to eliminate the situation of scarcity rents and high relative wages for skilled workers. Therefore, it is worth inquiring why the SENAI has not had a greater impact on skilled-worker supply, both within São Paulo manufacturing as a whole and within the sector dealt with here.[63] The question is all the more interesting because the SENAI could have been an admirable instrument for a much greater contribution to industrial training. It generally has an excellent reputation for well-conceived and well-executed training programs, closely related to the needs of industry. Furthermore, the SENAI avoids a serious potential problem for widescale "general" training by industry—the possibility of productivity gains generated by the training firm but appropriated as an external economy by other companies. Under the SENAI, all firms must contribute to training workers who then enter the general labor force, where they are available to all employers.

Availability of facilities for training has been the major limitation to the SENAI's expansion; for, on the demand side, there have usually been several applicants for every place available. Lack of training facilities, in turn, stems from lack of resources allocated to the SENAI. The SENAI's 1-percent industrial payroll tax has amounted to approximately 0.2 percent of the value added in

61. This was computed from data on SENAI activities and on the São Paulo skilled labor force. These data are available in *Boletim do Centro de Estudos "Roberto Mange,"* no. 25 (São Paulo, 1962).

62. This is based upon interviews with plant managers and personnel directors in the sector.

63. This question of the relation of the SENAI's program to the overall task of training the Brazilian industrial labor force has rarely been posed. In the light of its impressive individual training projects, the typical attitude has been one of self-congratulation. See, e.g., E. S. Fischlowitz, "Manpower Problems in Brazil," *International Labour Review* (April 1959), p. 417.

industry. These revenues have not been adequate for training an industrial labor force which between 1946 and 1963 increased at an annual compound rate of 4.5 percent.[64]

Lack of money has particularly affected the supply of training for the skills required by the sector under study here. In an effort to maximize the number of workers trained with its limited resources, the SENAI has concentrated on skills which require less costly equipment for instruction. (This, rather than an effort to maximize increased productivity from available training expenditure, even though it might be concentrated on a much smaller number of workers, seems to be the SENAI's policy.) Consequently, the heavy-engineering sector, with its relatively expensive machine tools, has been penalized, for the SENAI has directed its efforts to other industries and, within the mechanical industry, largely to light-machinery skills.

The SENAI's budgetary system has been another reason for the inadequacy of its efforts. Because resources for training are based on industrial payrolls and the volume of manufacturing output, the supply of training is a function of previous production. Consequently, unless training costs per worker are decreasing, the supply of skilled workers cannot increase more rapidly than lagged output, and thus cannot correct an initial scarcity situation that may have existed.

It is not enough to cite the SENAI's insufficient resources, however, for measures could well have been taken to remedy the deficiency. What seems to lie at the root of the situation is the fact that Brazilian industrialists, who would have to pay the bill for an expanded SENAI program, have not been willing to do so. Even though they are generally satisfied with the quality of the SENAI's work, and even though there is no problem of unappropriated externalities, they have not felt a real need to expand its facilities. Despite verbal protestations about the need for more training, in practice they have been content with what has been in fact the major source of training: the learning generated as a by-product of production.

LEARNING-BY-DOING

The sector's most important source of training has been workers' learning of their skills on the job. Some 50 percent of the sector's

64. Computed from data in *SENAI Relatório*, p. 8.

highly qualified workers (*oficiais*) have acquired their skills solely through work experience.[65] The training process has operated in the following manner. Unskilled workers enter the factory force and begin work as helpers (*ajudantes*). Assisting the skilled workers, they have a good opportunity to observe how various tasks are performed. After a few months, helpers are given small tasks—for example, minor welding or machining jobs—in the company of skilled workers. As semiskilled jobs become vacant within the firm, workers of ability and motivation move into such positions and gradually progress to jobs of increasing technical difficulty, under the supervision and informal instruction of the skilled workers and master workmen. Moving up the ladder of small skill improvements as machinists or welders, they receive wage increases in accordance with their skill progress.

A similar process operates for workers who enter the firm as semiskilled workers, often on the basis of learning and experience gained in small workshops or other firms. Beginning at their original skill level, some are able to progress to more difficult tasks until they attain fully qualified (*oficial*) positions.

Firms believe that the costs of training by this process are very low. Because foremen and supervisors generally have a great deal of unoccupied time on the shop floor, as they await possible technical or production problems, the opportunity cost to the firm for their *ad hoc* technical instruction is minimal. Costs that might be incurred through damage to equipment or work-in-progress are also believed to be low. Workers are not moved to tasks where they might cause such losses until they have demonstrated competence at previous skill levels. This smooth transition is possible because tasks proceed on a continuous range of increasing technical complexity, along which the worker is always under the supervision of other skilled workers and the group supervisor. Hence costs are held to a minimum; and through this process, training is "spun-off" as a by-product of the production of commodities.

Training times required for this process vary, but in general workers can assimilate the skills to move up a notch within the skill-pay hierarchy in six weeks to a few months.[66] A bigger step, from

65. This information came from interviews with foremen and personnel directors in the sector.

66. What follows is based upon interviews with foremen, production managers, and training directors of the sector.

ordinary machinist to highly qualified toolmaker, for example, may take two to three years. Since many workers are progressing simultaneously, however, additional skilled personnel at all levels are generated in a few months, as everyone on the ladder moves a small step. The "spin-off" rate is essentially a function of the demand for skilled personnel, which pulls people up the ladder, and of the training mechanism, the volume of value added, subject to the constraint of the learning possibilities inherent in the production process.

Firms take it as a matter of course that their needs for skilled bench workers are supplied by this mechanism. To test whether the data actually indicate a statistically significant relation, and if so, how much learning was associated with how much doing, a double-log regression equation was estimated for spin-off in the São Paulo metalworking industries in the period 1955–1963. The annual increment to the stock of skilled workers who had not acquired training through formal training or apprenticeship programs was taken as the dependent variable, and value added in these industries in the previous year, Q_{t-1}, was the independent variable.[67] Eight observations were available, and the estimated regression equation, in double log form, is

$$\log (S_t - S_{t-1}) = 0.9235 \log (Q_{t-1}).$$

The corrected R^2 is 0.63, and both the F-test and the t-test are significant above the 1-percent level. The Durbin-Watson statistic is 2.25. This equation indicates that a rise in the industry's value added in one year was, in the subsequent year, followed by a nearly equal rise in the number of skilled workers supplied from

67. This regression equation was computed with the following data and procedures. A time series on value added in the São Paulo State metalworking industries 1954–1962 was constructed from data in IBGE, *Produção Industrial Brasileira* (Rio de Janeiro, 1960); from the *Censo Industrial;* and from IBRD, "Manufacturing Industry", "Current Economic Position and Prospects of Brazil," vol. 5, mimeographed [Washington, D.C., February 1965], Appendix A, p. 2. A time series on the number of *qualificados* in these industries, 1955–1963, was computed from data in the *SENAI Relatório.* From this, annual increments in the industry's skilled work force were calculated. On the basis of interviews with personnel directors of firms in this industry, it was assumed that 40% of the additional skilled workers had acquired their training through the SENAI or other formal training programs. The remainder constituted the series on spin-off, which was regressed against the production time series. The first results gave an intercept which was not statistically significant, and the equation was estimated again, eliminating the intercept. Taking time as the independent variable, to see if these increases in skilled-worker supply could be accounted for simply by a trend factor, gave a poorer statistical fit.

spin-off. During this period this mechanism operated to generate annual increases in skilled-worker supply in a range of 8–12 percent.

We should note some of the conditions which have made possible this process of skill formation. First, the high wage differential between skilled and unskilled workers has constituted a direct incentive for learning new skills. Secondly, the learning process has been greatly facilitated by the fact that the necessary skills are ranged along a relatively continuous spectrum, so that the worker can move along by small steps to attain higher qualifications. This process has also required a modicum of mechanical aptitude and intelligence on the part of workers, so that they could assimilate skills without elaborate instruction. In this connection, we should note that all employers, both foreign and domestic, emphasize what they consider the unusual capacity of Brazilian workers for rapid learning of mechanical skills.[68] There have also been no institutional barriers to workers learning new skills and entering better-paid jobs upon qualification. Limitations that in other countries might be imposed by restrictive work rules or a strong crafts-union tradition have been notably absent.[69]

In effect, the factory has functioned as a school for vocational training. Teaching has been provided by the skilled workers, foremen, and the work experience itself. Equipment for instruction has been supplied by the firm, for its normal production needs. Indeed, the factory workers have had machinery which was too expensive for the SENAI's vocational schools. And—an important advantage over many formal training programs—workers have been paid a wage on which to live during the period when they were undergoing training.

This training has also been closely related to the actual needs of

68. I could not find any material comparing the mechanical aptitude of Brazilian workers with that of workers in other countries to substantiate or negate this claim; but in light of the importance of the supply of training for economic development, this would be an excellent subject for further study by industrial psychologists. It might also be worthwhile to investigate the possibilities for generalizing from this Brazilian experience by research into the social and psychological conditions that have been associated with this learning in the course of production. For example, anthropologists might consider the conditions of recruitment into the labor force and the existence within the factory of an environment supporting such learning.

69. The sector's union, the metalworkers, is organized on an industrial basis. Although as one of Brazil's strongest unions it might have been able to limit entry, the union has been chiefly concerned with maintaining real wages in the midst of the inflation. Perhaps because of the general expansionary climate that has followed constant economic growth and demand for skilled workers, there has been no effort at restricting entry to specific trades or to higher skill levels.

industry, so that the problems encountered in some formal training programs in less-developed countries have been avoided.[70] In those efforts, elaborate training facilities were provided, but the results were disappointing. The skills taught were not always those demanded in the labor market; and the schools were sometimes too far removed from the actual production process to prepare trainees for industrial life. As suggested below, learning-by-doing may be inefficient in other respects, but it has avoided the failures of poorly implemented vocational training.

In a final evaluation of learning-by-doing, however, we should compare its costs with those of alternative training mechanisms. As noted above, firms believe that this process is virtually costless. Better accounting might revise their estimate, though they are certain that production equipment and output are seldom damaged. Nevertheless, whatever its other virtues, learning-by-doing has its social costs, in the worker's lower productivity during the extended "training" period. Because of the lack of a concentrated instructional focus, learning-by-doing is a relatively inefficient method of training.

We gain a rough idea of this inefficiency from an illustrative comparison of the costs involved in transforming a machinist into a highly qualified toolmaker. As mentioned earlier, it would take approximately two years for the worker to assimilate the requisite skills in the course of the production process. During this period, his annual earnings would be approximately 300 *contos* (as of mid-1964) below what he could be earning at the higher skill level.[71] Applying a 10-percent discount rate to the 300 *contos* of annual productivity and earnings differential over two years, this gives a cost of 513 *contos*. By contrast, in an intensive vocational training program in which the same instruction could be provided in two months, the costs, including earnings foregone, are approximately 207 *contos*, or less than half as much.[72] In this perspective, learning-by-doing may have "done the job" of providing skilled workers, but it did so relatively expensively. Given the unwillingness of the industrialists to expand the SENAI and given the

70. See Frederick Harbison and Charles A. Myers, *Education, Manpower and Economic Growth* (New York, 1964), p. 56.

71. Information comes from foremen and personnel directors in the sector.

72. See n. 54 above.

absence of government-sponsored training programs during this period, the more efficient training was simply not forthcoming.[73]

CONCLUSIONS

THE EXPERIENCE OF THE SECTOR

Despite the relatively high educational and skill requirements needed for the manufacture of heavy-engineering equipment, supply of these inputs has not posed a serious barrier to this sector's expansion. First, there has been considerable saving of educational inputs. The Brazilian skilled workers have less than a third of the formal schooling of their American counterparts. The sector also uses less than half as many engineers per unit of output as the American machinery industry. Such educational saving has not prevented the sector from attaining output of high quality and (with equivalent production equipment) productivity comparable to American levels. Moreover, lower formal-education levels have not inhibited the sector's flexibility in adopting new and more complex technology, for in the past decade firms successfully changed to heavier equipment and new product lines. The sector's experience in economizing formal educational inputs indicates that the elasticity of substitution between education and other inputs, in response to different relative factor-prices, is greater than is assumed in a rigid "manpower requirements" approach to education and development.

Even after such adjustments on the demand side, the sector's demand for human capital inputs are among the highest in Brazilian industry. Because of the dynamic supply response to increased demands for skilled manpower, however, these demands have been met with supply sufficiently elastic to avoid any seriously inhibiting effect on the sector's rapid (10–15 percent per annum) rate of growth.

The sector was able to begin production, as we saw, with skills generated in various seedbed activities found even in a predominantly agricultural economy, and with immigrants and expatriates from industrially more advanced countries. Once output began,

73. In 1964, the Federal Ministry of Education began an accelerated program of industrial training that attempted to train 50,000 skilled workers of various grades at a total cost of approximately $2,000,000. Data on this program are available in *Ensino Industrial*, 3, no. 7.

the number of domestic skilled personnel also grew rapidly. Specific production skills and experience have been supplied largely as the result of the learning generated in the course of production, that is, as a by-product of normal production activities. For foremen and supervisors, this has been complemented by formal instruction, primarily in design reading. Some individuals have on their own been able to respond to the high return to training investment created by a high relative wage for skilled personnel. In cases where firms perceived that they could gain by increasing the supply of skilled personnel, they too have maintained formal training programs. Vocational training has also been supported by industry under legal compulsion, through the SENAI. By these various training mechanisms, in the years 1951–1963 the number of skilled workers in the metalworking industries of São Paulo State rose from approximately 24,700 to 75,000, at an annual cumulative rate of 10.4 percent.

The supply of engineering personnel has also grown rapidly, as we saw, at an 8.7-percent compound rate over 21 years. The supply of technically educated personnel seems to have been responding to the social and economic changes occurring in Brazil since the 1929 coffee crisis and subsequent accelerated industrialization. With the social restratification that accompanied industrialization, demands for education increased as individuals sought higher qualification as an avenue to higher positions. This crisis of the traditional society was accompanied by far-reaching changes in the country's intellectual and educational traditions as technical accomplishments and subjects, which were considered more appropriate for a modernizing society, came into favor. The achievements of Brazilian industrialization gave increasing validity to these themes and helped orient individuals into engineering careers.

These social factors have been solidly reinforced by economic conditions affecting the supply of engineering personnel. High relative wages for engineers have provided a sizable return to investment in technical education. In response to these conditions, the demand for engineering education increased rapidly enough to permit the large increases in engineer supply that we have noted. Indeed, the excess demand for engineering education suggests that supply would have increased even more had the educational system been able to keep pace with student demands. Similar economic conditions were associated with a marked change in the pattern of student specialization in the São Paulo engineering schools. Within eight years, the percentage of students specializing in the newer engineering fields almost doubled, with concomitant halving of concentration in civil engineering and architecture. Again, supply seems to have been responding to changes in demand and the development, with import-substitution, of effective market demand for mechanical products and their inputs.

These changes came after years of polemic and claims, dating at least from the 1920's, that "too few" engineers were being graduated and that the engineering students had an "excessive" preference for specialization in civil engineering rather than newer "industrial" fields. While the number of engineers was criticized as "insufficient," however, the engineers who were graduated in the 1920's and 1930's often had trouble finding jobs.[74] At the same time, since the main source of engineering employment was in construction, the preference for civil engineering studies is understandable. Therefore it seems that the supply of engineers was being blamed for demand conditions—the absence of a large industrial sector with its associated demand for engineers. In fact, when, with accelerated industrialization, demand for engineers changed, the pattern of supply also adjusted.

This experience conforms with Myint's suggestion: "The problems of creating . . . demand for trained personnel may be even more important than the problem of creating the supply by investment in 'social capital.' Given the demand, the supply of trained personnel of most types . . . would seem to respond more automatically and to a greater extent than is usually allowed for."[75]

As noted earlier, certain social conditions—particularly the relative absence of institutional barriers in the labor market—were necessary for educational supply to adjust effectively to demand conditions. The picture in São Paulo contrasts with another model of educational supply, which assumes that "The individual . . . is born into an elevator of educational progress [which leaves him at a] predetermined educational and socio-

74. This information is from interviews with engineers graduated from Brazilian engineering schools during the 1930's.
75. Hla Myint, "An Interpretation of Economic Backwardness," reprinted in *The Economics of Underdevelopment*, ed. Agarwala and Singh, pp. 104–105.

economic level." Such rigid conditions may "accord closely with social and educational reality" in some countries. But in São Paulo, with real possibilities for upward mobility, the prospect of high returns could provide an effective incentive for individuals to acquire higher qualifications and change "predetermined" educational and social structures.[76]

Increases in the number of engineers graduated answered only part of the firms' needs, for they also needed engineers with specialized skills and production experience. In their initial activities, firms often hired expatriates with the highly specific skills they required. They have also created their own domestic supply by the experience generated in the course of production and by training programs. The latter have been worthwhile for individual companies, as we noted, because imperfect labor mobility and oligopsonistic market conditions have enabled them to recover their costs by sharing in the increased productivity of trained personnel. In these cases, pressures on the labor market have been alleviated, since the same firm that was generating additional demand for skilled personnel was also providing for increased supply.

Evidence indicates that firms have been satisfied with the flow of skilled personnel available from these sources. Training programs rank low within the hierarchy of the firms' concerns, and are generally under the administration of low-echelon executives. Further evidence of lack of any great concern is seen in the fact that companies have not felt the need to have the SENAI's vocational training activities expanded. This cannot be attributed to lack of political access or to a communications gap between industry and government, for the SENAI is administered by the Federation of Industries. Rather, though firms are satisfied with the quality of the SENAI's work, they have not felt themselves sufficiently pressed by shortages of skilled workers to pay for more training.

Furthermore, firms have not hesitated to establish their plants far from the existing pools of skilled labor in São Paulo City. In these cases, other advantages were more important to management than the training problem that they created for themselves by locating away from readily available supplies of skilled labor. Nor

76. The quotations are from John Vaizey, "The Labour Market and the Economic Forecaster," *International Labour Review* (April 1964), pp. 367–368.

did high manpower requirements deter firms from entering this sector. Indeed, as noted earlier, attracted by favorable market prospects, they even *over*-invested in this sector.

The relatively high benefit/cost ratios for investment in engineer education and training for shop workers suggest that there may well be under-investment in the supply of some of the human resources required by this sector and other Brazilian mechanical industries.[77] Institutional rigidities have prevented more rapid expansion of the engineering schools, and capital market imperfections have limited investment by shop personnel in higher qualifications. As the rapidly expanding output of these industries indicates, however, scarcity of skilled personnel has not placed a physical constraint on production. Rather, scarcity has meant only that these inputs have been supplied under (needlessly) high cost conditions. The price of these inputs, moreover, is not as important a determinant of total costs as the price of other inputs such as steel or unskilled labor.[78] And, even paying scarcity rents for these factors, firms of the sector have been able to meet world market prices for their products.[79] In this perspective, skilled personnel appears as an input which, because of insufficient processing facilities, is unnecessarily expensive. Because of the very low price of its raw material—unskilled and uneducated human labor—this input's final price is still cheap enough to permit its users to compete effectively.

SOME GENERAL IMPLICATIONS

The sector's experience in encountering elastic supply of skilled manpower has not been unique nor has it been a case of a sector

77. The existence of scarcity conditions despite the large increases in supply of skilled manpower is similar to the case of electrical power in Brazil. Between 1949 and 1962, power production increased at an annual compound rate of 10.4%. (Calculated from data in Baer, *Economic Development in Brazil*, Statistical Appendix, Table C-3; and Banco do Brasil, *Relatório de 1963* [Rio de Janeiro, 1964], p. 285.) Such sustained increases in supply might be highly satisfactory in less dynamic economies, but in Brazil demand pressed ahead so rapidly that severe electricity shortages continued.

78. Even in this sector, with its unusually high engineer input, the effects of the high supply curve for engineers on total costs are relatively small. Since labor costs constitute approximately one-third of the sector's total costs and engineer wages are about one-third of all labor costs, a 10% rise in the salary of engineers means a 1% increase in total costs.

79. We cannot discuss here the effects of engineer scarcity at the macro-level, but we should note that despite the scarcity rents paid to engineers, Brazil has well-developed mechanical, automotive, chemical, and pharmaceutical industries, all of which have relatively high engineer inputs.

growing at the expense of other industries.[80] During the same period, all the metalworking industries of São Paulo State were able to find the skilled manpower to grow at similarly high rates. Beginning from a base of value added of approximately 395 million dollars in 1949, the São Paulo metalworking industries expanded their output at a cumulative annual rate of 11.0 percent through 1959.[81] The skilled work-force of these industries grew at similarly high rates—an annual increase of 10.4 percent.[82] The simultaneous expansion of these industries indicates that the dynamic supply of trained manpower may be elastic for annual increases as high as 8–12 percent. The regression equation on spin-off presented earlier indicates that in this range, increases in the metalworking industries' output were followed by nearly equal increases in the supply of skills from learning-by-doing. This experience argues strongly against the contention that ambitious investment programs may soon encounter external diseconomies of inelastic skill supply.[83] With workers able to progress to higher skill levels within a three-month period (either by moving along the ladder of learning in the course of production or through formal training programs), thus making possible such large annual increases in the skilled labor force, a development program would probably be constrained sooner by the availability of investment funds than by the supply of skilled manpower.

Furthermore, as we saw, these increases in factor supply were largely in dynamic response to expanding demand in earlier periods. The improvement in the education and skills of the Brazilian labor force appears as the result of the higher income levels and the industrial experience created by rapid economic growth, rather than a "prerequisite" which had to come before economic development.[84] This experience suggests that an under-

80. Although there was a constant drain of skilled personnel from the smaller mechanical firms to the larger ones, additional skilled workers have been generated fast enough to make possible the rapid growth rates cited for the mechanical industry as a whole.

81. This is based on calculations using the data on value added in the São Paulo mechanical, transportation-equipment, electrical-material, and metallurgical industries as given in the *Censo Industrial*. The exchange-rate used for the conversion to dollars was the average import rate.

82. Computed from *SENAI Relatório*, p. 9.

83. Fleming, "External Economies."

84. In the case of skilled manpower the sector's experience supports a point which Alexander Gerschenkron has emphasized with regard to capital and entrepreneurship: the

developed country contemplating investment programs in sectors with high skill requirements need not be deterred by present low skill levels in its work-force. In the Brazilian case, the sequence was from an expansion of production, in response to demands in the product market, to an improvement in the quality of the labor force via the built-in mechanisms we have discussed.

---

possibility of "patterns of substitution" rather than binding preconditions for development. See his "Reflections on the Concept of 'Prerequisites' of Modern Industrialization" and "The Approach to European Industrialization: A Postscript," especially pages 357–359, in *Economic Backwardness in Historical Perspective* (Cambridge, Mass., 1962).

IV

KNOW-HOW

The supply of complex technology, or "know-how," has been a matter for serious concern to Brazilian economists and policy-makers.[1] First, they have feared that Brazilian firms lack the capabilities for developing such know-how themselves. Further-more, it is felt that there are obstacles to the international transfer of technology, and that Brazilian industry—particularly companies under domestic ownership—has had serious difficulties in importing know-how from the advanced countries. These concerns, in turn, are given important macro-economic implications. During the early 1960's, for example, it was often suggested in Brazil that rapid economic development had previously been possible because it had been based on import substitution of technically "easy" products. Further growth, however, would be much more problematic, because it would involve production of technically "complex" products.

Concern about the supply of advanced technical capacity has also been voiced in another manner, namely, in the complaint that Brazilian firms do too little research and development work on their own. The extensive use that Brazilian firms have, in fact, made of licensing agreements to import know-how is considered to entail a social misallocation of resources. Although this proposi-tion may not appear obvious, it has been accepted as self-evident by many Brazilian economists and policymakers since the early 1960's. Basic to their concern has been the fear of permanent colonial status resulting from dependence on the highly developed countries for one of the most important inputs to the modernization process—advanced science and technology. Such anxieties have been given "technical" support by the work of John Kendrick and others on the importance of technological progress in promoting economic growth in the United States. These findings have been

1. For an expression of similar concerns for economic development in Latin America as a whole, see Victor Urquidi, *The Challenge of Development in Latin America* (New York, 1964), pp. 106–111.

interpreted in Brazil to indicate that the country should greatly increase its allocations both for scientific research and for industrial development work. In early 1964 these attitudes were incorporated into public policy, when the Brazilian government curtailed foreign-exchange allocations for royalty payments, in an effort to abrogate overseas licensing agreements and compel private entrepreneurs to do more research and development.

Although the supply of advanced technology is believed to have major importance for economic development, relatively little empirical material on the subject is available.[2] Consequently, it may be useful here to discuss these questions in a specific context— how these problems have been dealt with in the growth of the Brazilian heavy-engineering products sector.

"COMPLEX TECHNOLOGY"

As the expression is used in Brazil, "complex" or "advanced" technology seems to have two principal economic characteristics. The production of goods involving such technology requires special labor skills for high-quality work in fabrication and assembly. These skill requirements were discussed in the previous chapter. As regards know-how, "complex technology" refers to knowledge far from the general fund of information which is available relatively easily and cheaply to businessmen and engineers. Because this know-how relates to highly specialized production activities, for which markets are limited, only a few firms have carried out the research and generated the experience necessary to acquire it.

Embodied in patents, trade secrets, and specialized experience, such know-how entails special costs for newcomer firms. To generate this knowledge by their own development work, they must invest in the research and production needed for learning. Alternatively, they may attempt to purchase the know-how from firms

2. See I. Svennilson's comments to this effect in "The Transfer of Industrial Know-How to Non-Industrialized Countries," in *Economic Development with Special Reference to East Asia: Proceedings of a Conference held by the International Economics Association*, ed. K. Berrill (New York, 1964). Raymond Vernon has also remarked on the scanty data available on the working of licensing agreements. See his paper, "Problems and Prospects in the Export of Manufactured Goods from the Less-Developed Countries" (Expert Paper No. 2 [United Nations Conference on Trade and Development, 1964]), pp. 16–17. Urquidi (*The Challenge of Development*) does not discuss licensing agreements at all.

which already have it. As mentioned, both possibilities have been
a source of major concern to Brazilian policymakers. First, they
have feared that Brazilian industrialists and engineers lack the
technical capacity to develop such know-how on their own. Second,
if Brazilian firms attempt to purchase know-how abroad, it is
believed that they face a highly oligopolistic market structure, a
consequence of the limited size of the market for highly specialized
products and hence the small number of firms with the requisite
know-how. The foreign companies' market power may enable them
either to withhold supply completely or else to demand very high
prices, impeding the development of new producers. Let us now
consider how these problems have actually been resolved in the
growth of this sector.

DEMAND AND SUPPLY OF COMPLEX TECHNOLOGY

As we saw in Chapter II, a major theme in the sector's history
has been entry into new and usually more complex product lines.
Because of the nonspecificity of the sector's fabricating technology,
all that was usually needed to turn out a new product were the
technical specifications and sometimes instruction in fabrication
techniques. This pattern of expansion into more technically
complex product lines has been intensified in recent years, as
excess capacity induced many firms, domestic and foreign, to
develop new products.

In the sector's early days, necessary know-how was supplied
largely from the engineering abilities of the firms' owner-managers,
perhaps complemented by the experience of an immigrant or
expatriate engineer. Another source of supply was the Institute of
Technological Research of the São Paulo Polytechnical School.
The Institute's consulting services enabled firms to overcome the
indivisibilities which might otherwise have precluded their access
to research carried on by a large staff using expensive laboratory
facilities. Such domestic supply has continued in recent years; for
projects that have not entailed a major discontinuity from existing
products, the sector's firms or their clients have generally developed
their own designs. These have been based on their experience with
existing equipment installations, on the knowledge available
through engineering journals, and on their own professional ability

to design necessary equipment. The technical capacity of domestic engineering staffs has increased greatly in the course of time, and products which previously involved an important departure from existing knowledge have subsequently been assimilated into their own experience. Thus, for example, while the designs for Brazil's first steel-making equipment were beyond the capacity of domestic engineers and were purchased abroad, projects for some recently constructed rolling mills and blast furnaces were developed by local personnel.

Know-how that the sector's firms lack and do not consider advantageous to develop themselves has been imported from the advanced countries. Subsidiaries of international corporations usually acquire their know-how directly from their home company, though in the numerous cases when the Brazilian subsidiary has entered new and different product lines, they have also concluded agreements with other companies. Firms under Brazilian ownership and management have also imported know-how in two principal forms. On some occasions, firms have simply purchased designs, either from a consulting firm specializing in such engineering projects, or from a manufacturing firm willing, for a fee, to supply designs and use of its trademark. In other cases, firms have entered into more extensive "technical assistance" agreements, where in addition to designs, the licensing firm provides technical instruction, both by opening its facilities to trainees and by supplying personnel as specialized instructors in the Brazilian plant.

Using designs purchased from abroad, however, has not absolved firms from doing a great deal of technical work themselves. The usual procedure in such cases is for the overseas firm to supply the general project specifications. The details and adaptation to local raw materials and special preferences of the client are generally done by the Brazilian firm's staff.[3] Such work is within the technical capacity of domestic engineers, and their work is generally cheaper than imported designs. Local engineers also have the advantage of being close to the client for whom the project is being tailored. For these reasons, the sector's firms have made extensive use of Brazilian staff even on projects supplied through licensing agreements. When

3. For example, Brazilian steel has a carbon content and structural characteristics different from the raw material specified by foreign designs, so that redesigning with different dimensions is often necessary.

firms do not have large "research and development" divisions, such work is usually carried out by engineers in deparments such as sales or production, or is handled by senior management personnel. Imported and domestic know-how have been complementary rather than competitive, and demands for the former generally increased demands for the latter.

LICENSING AGREEMENTS: THE MARKET AND THE TERMS

The international market for know-how has not in fact placed the sector's firms in a weak bargaining position. In the case of technical knowledge supplied by consulting firms, there are usually several competing companies in different countries from whom clients can choose. For know-how supplied by firms engaged primarily in production activities, however, other potentially complicating factors are added. Because transfer of technical capacity might reduce the overseas firm's product sales, a serious imperfection may be introduced into the market for know-how. Furthermore, if only a few firms have the know-how related to highly specialized production activities, they may be able to negotiate from a very strong position.

The sector's experience, however, has been that even in narrowly delimited production activities, there are usually several firms in the world with the requisite know-how, and so pure monopoly or highly oligopolistic situations are almost always avoided.[4] Moreover, in bargaining with foreign production firms, the sector's companies have generally been able to benefit from conditions which strengthen their own position. The alternatives before a firm from which a license is sought are: (a) to open a manufacturing subsidiary in Brazil; or (b) to see its return from know-how, based on export sales, go to zero if other firms with the necessary know-how do negotiate a licensing agreement, or if they open a manufacturing subsidiary and dominate the Brazilian market.

Relying on the inaction of other companies to prevent the second

4. The ECLA mission which studied this sector and gave special attention to possible problems involved in transmission of technology cites only one case of oligopolistic market power impeding the transfer of technology—designs for certain cement-making equipment. According to the report, even this case was being resolved as a result of the market pressures cited below. See ECLA, *Basic Equipment in Brazil* (*The Manufacture of Industrial Machinery and Equipment in Brazil*, vol. 1 [New York: United Nations, 1963]), pp. 46–47.

possibility from materializing is risky, for a firm can rarely be sure of the overseas investment and licensing plans of its competitors. At the same time, the company which has been approached may find that several factors militate against opening a plant of its own in Brazil. The firm may not have sufficient capital or trained personnel to commit to such a venture. If it does have resources available, it may well prefer to allocate them in its home market, in other advanced countries, or in other less-developed countries. Either in response to such considerations or simply as a matter of "company policy," some firms in the advanced countries do not consider establishing overseas plants, but prefer to "go the licensing route" in adding to returns on their know-how. Consequently a would-be licensee firm may be able to negotiate with several potential licensing companies in the advanced countries.

Its bargaining position is further strengthened by the fact that the marginal cost of knowledge which has already been developed is close to zero. Hence the would-be licensee is offering the firm in the advanced country payment for a resource which costs it little, but for which, if no agreement is concluded, it receives nothing. In addition to protecting income in a disappearing export market, a licensing agreement may enable firms in the developed countries to *increase* their returns from know-how. The potential licensee may well have better facilities for penetrating the local market than the exporter. Because of locational advantages and the economies of spreading the fixed costs involved over a larger sales line, his distribution and service facilities may be more comprehensive. These factors, along with any import restrictions that may previously have repressed demand, may enable a local producer to develop a larger market than was available through exports. Under such conditions, the exporting firm can increase its profits if the increase in sales volume is large enough to offset any decline in the profit rate applied for know-how as opposed to the margin on sales.[5]

This seems to have been the reasoning of some overseas firms that have used licensing agreements with a strong local company to increase returns from a market which had previously been small

5. In cases where the firm in the advanced country was previously participating in a highly competitive export market, with intense pressures on profit margins, the difference between the previous margin and the new licensing rate may not be very great.

and sporadic. As a result of these conditions, the sector's firms have had no trouble finding companies in Western Europe and the United States to supply the know-how they required.[6]

Negotiating in this market, Brazilian firms have generally paid a charge of 5 percent of the sales price of the product fabricated under the license. In cases of highly specialized knowledge they have paid more, occasionally as much as 10 percent, while for know-how in which their own development costs would not be very high, they have paid 1 to 3 percent. In addition to product designs, licensees have also received use of the foreign firm's trademark (and have assumed the obligation of maintaining its quality standards). This has been an important selling advantage. In cases of more extensive technical assistance, upon payment of the additional expenses involved, Brazilian firms have gained general access to the licensing firm's experience and facilities, enabling them to recruit production and training experts. Finally, in addition to royalty payments, licensing agreements have generally included clauses prohibiting Brazilian firms from exporting to markets in which they might compete with the licensing firm. On occasion, however, hard bargaining by a Brazilian firm has enabled it to retain export rights, for example, for the Latin America Free Trade Area. This has been much easier when negotiating with firms which, for internal reasons, do not pursue an aggressive export policy, at least in some geographical regions.

LICENSING AGREEMENTS VERSUS DOMESTIC RESEARCH AND DEVELOPMENT

When the sector's firms are asked why, for technical knowledge involving a major discontinuity with their previous work, they have preferred to import know-how rather than develop it themselves, they usually reply that such a procedure would be "too difficult," "too expensive," or "too slow." That is, relative price conditions may make it economical for a Brazilian firm to acquire its know-how by paying royalties. Research and development in Brazil may well be more expensive than in the advanced countries because of a higher supply price for certain key inputs. In particular, Brazilian firms may lack highly specialized technical training and experience,

---

6. An even freer market in know-how would develop if the Iron Curtain countries were to participate more actively as sellers.

which indeed may not be available in Brazil without importation. Firms in the advanced countries, however, may have these factors available at a lower cost because they have already engaged in the production that generates specialized experience. Moreover, in the developed countries, the size of the market for specialized personnel and other research inputs may also be large enough to justify local production, and permit supply at costs lower than in Brazil.

Furthermore, if there are significant economies of scale in development work—either for the research and development sector as a whole or for the individual project—and if the Brazilian market is too small for optimal scale activity, then importation may be cheaper than domestic supply. In addition, development work often involves high fixed costs for expensive laboratories and perhaps pilot-plant facilities. These may be economical in the advanced countries, where costs can be spread over a large sales volume, but they may not be justified in the smaller Brazilian market. These considerations apply especially to capital goods producers, whose demand for particular products is both limited and uncertain. Under such conditions, firms prefer the variable costs of paying royalties as sales occur to the high sunken costs of research work which can be spread only over a small and un-predictable market.

Even if these conditions are offset by other factors, so that the costs of research and development work are competitive in Brazil, comparative advantage may dictate importing know-how, and concentrating available capital and engineering personnel in direct production activities. If rates of return in Brazilian manu-facturing activities are higher than in the advanced countries, firms maximize profits by allocating their inputs for production and importing their know-how, developed by companies whose resources did not have equally high opportunity costs.

Furthermore, know-how has a unique feature that makes it of special advantage for international trade, and influences Brazilian firms in their allocation of resources between production and development work. Once developed, know-how can be supplied at low marginal cost, particularly if, as noted above, the firm in the developed country will in any case lose its export market for this product. This contrasts with other commodities, which must be produced for each sale, so that price conditions may be less favorable for trade. Although the firm in the advanced country can supply know-how at low marginal costs, the prospective licensee must contemplate its alternative of high research and development costs. Hence a wide margin for bargaining is opened, whose limits are set on the one hand by the cost of rediscovering technical knowledge, and on the other by the prospective supplier's alternative, getting nothing for his know-how. In this range of negotiation, the licensee may be able to acquire know-how at a price much lower than his own prospective development costs.

Another factor frequently cited by firms of the sector when they explain their decision to enter into licensing agreements is the saving in time involved. With a licensing agreement, they can acquire the know-how they need almost immediately, in contrast with the longer waiting period involved in independent development work. Firms want to reduce uncertainty about the length of the development process, and they wish to minimize the chance that a competitor might enter the new market before they do. Firms can also earn higher returns to the extent that their resources are employed much sooner in the new product line rather than being employed during a research period in activities yielding lower returns. In reducing the risks and uncertainty of the development process and in gaining a higher return on capital and other factors by shifting them immediately to a more profitable activity, the Brazilian firms can take advantage of an option which is not available to firms in the advanced countries, who must seek new market opportunities at the technical-commercial frontiers.

Finally, firms have sometimes concluded licensing agreements in order to enjoy the selling advantages of a well-known trademark.[7] Because licensing firms have generally insisted that their standards be maintained, clients have considered an established trademark as a guarantee of quality. This has been especially important in the heavy-engineering sector's competition, because demand has been relatively price-inelastic with respect to higher quality.

7. These considerations also apply to "patent licensing," where a fee is paid not for blueprints—which are available anyhow as published patent materials—but for providing the legal monopoly to use them. In such cases, the firms consider that the market advantage conferred by the exclusive right to use such know-how is acquired more economically by paying royalties than through internal research work to develop a comparable product.

Although for all these reasons firms in the sector have often imported know-how, they have not taken a slavish approach to the question of licensing agreements versus internal research and development. When, in the middle and late 1950's, some firms concluded numerous and extensive licensing agreements, others were more dubious of their value and wary of the costs that royalty payments might add to their contract bids. Hence they concluded agreements for fewer products, often only for specific components, and did not hesitate to cancel them if experience indicated they were not gaining the advantages they had expected. These different firms meet in the sharp market competition that, as described in Chapter VII, prevails in the sector; on any contract tender, there are bids from firms that have drawn their know-how from different sources, domestic and foreign. Therefore, firms with licensing agreements cannot simply shift their royalty payments to clients. Unless the cost of imported know-how is justified either as lower than domestic development costs or as compensated by other advantages, such as raw-material savings or higher productivity, they will lose in competition. As a result, a possible distortion in the market for imported know-how—that is, uncritical purchase of foreign know-how that might be more advantageously supplied domestically—is reduced.

EFFECTS OF LICENSING AGREEMENTS

Licensing agreements negotiated by the sector's firms have permitted manufacture of some products more quickly and at lower costs than would have been possible had firms had to rely on know-how they supplied themselves. Moreover, in cases where imported know-how constituted a true bottleneck input which could not have been supplied from domestic resources—for example, for lack of highly specialized technical knowledge or production experience—it was only this imported know-how that permitted production of these goods to get under way at all. To the extent, then, that the resources used in production would otherwise have been employed less productively, imported know-how permitted a net addition to output.

Imported know-how has also reduced monopoly power in the sector's market structure. Open access to specialized technical capacity through licensing agreements has reduced what might otherwise be significant imperfections in the market for this input, imperfections that would in turn distort the product market. The foreign firms might acquire know-how from their home companies, and some domestic firms with exceptionally gifted owner-managers might generate it themselves. Preferential access to this input would then permit such firms to enjoy monopoly positions in product lines which other companies could not enter for lack of the requisite know-how. Generalized availability of technical capacity through licensing agreements has, in fact, greatly reduced the monopoly power which some favored firms previously exercised.

Licensing agreements have also permitted the domestic firms to compete with the sector's international companies without inferiority in technical capacity. Indeed, as noted in Chapter II, the domestic firms have generally demonstrated better market performance than the foreign companies in the excess-capacity situation that developed in the sector after 1960. As a channel for acquiring specialized know-how, licensing agreements have also provided an alternative to direct foreign investment, for example, by opening domestic firms to foreign capital participation. Many Brazilians regard such a development with considerable reserve, but firms might otherwise be impelled to it for lack of other economical sources of advanced technology.

Another consequence of importing know-how has been an important increase in domestic technical capacity. As pointed out earlier, specialized knowledge and production experience are themselves an important input to the research and development process. By beginning manufacture of certain products on the basis of imported know-how, the domestic firms have gained competence and self-confidence in areas which were previously a mystery to them, so that they have been able subsequently to dispense with licensing agreements. For example, some high-pressure boiler equipment, electric furnaces, and steel-making equipment, for which designs previously had to be purchased abroad, are now designed by Brazilian engineers. Newly acquired technical capacity has also enabled the firms to absorb imported know-how in other, more complex product lines previously beyond their capabilities.

Finally, we should note that the costs of importing know-how to the Brazilian economy have been much lower than is generally supposed.[8] In the period 1956–1960, the country's total annual payments overseas for "Administrative and Technical Assistance" and "Patents and Royalties" averaged $33.8 million.[9] This amounted to less than 2 percent of the total foreign-exchange payments during the period, and less than 10 percent of the total negative balance for services.

CONCLUSIONS

The picture presented above does not suggest that the Brazilian firms' reliance upon imported know-how rather than that generated through domestic research and development involves a misallocation of resources. As noted, firms do develop much of their know-how internally and they rely on imports only for technical capacity that they can obtain more cheaply, in terms of relative cost conditions and their comparative advantage, from abroad. There are no obvious reasons for imputing error to the sector's firms on these decisions. They follow a critical approach with regard to the gains from licensing agreements, an attitude enforced by the sector's active competition between those companies developing know-how themselves and those importing it.

The concern of some Brazilians that their country is doing "too little" research and development appears to have two roots: ignorance concerning the cost conditions that may make it advantageous to import know-how, and an uncritical transfer to Brazil of notions from the advanced countries about the importance of research and development as a source of growth and of new investment opportunities. Unlike companies in the developed countries, who can find more productive techniques only at the frontiers of technical knowledge, Brazilian firms can draw upon a whole range of untapped opportunities that have already been discovered.[10]

8. The magnitude of royalty payments and particularly their pressure on the balance of payments are commonly believed to be enormous. A very popular pamphlet published in 1963, *Um Día na Vida de Brasiliense*, by Paulo Guilherme Martins (São Paulo), presents a picture in which almost all manufactured products consumed by an upper-class Brazilian involve royalty payments, at exorbitant rates, to foreign firms.

9. Data for this statement and the others in this paragraph are computed from SUMOC statistics published in Hélio Schlittler Silva, "Commércio Exterior e Desenvolvimento Econômico do Brasil," *Revista Brasileira de Ciências Sociais*, 2, no. 1, Tables 1, 2, 9, 12.

10. For a strong emphasis on the potential advantages available in this respect to latecomers to industrialization, see Alexander Gerschenkron, "Economic Backwardness in Historical Perspective," in *The Progress of Underdeveloped Areas*, ed. Bert F. Hoselitz (Chicago, 1952).

Furthermore, the problem of growth is very different in a Keynesian economy (potentially lacking investment outlets) and an inflationary economy like Brazil's, usually operating at capacity levels and with no deficiency in aggregate demand.

The sector's experience also suggests that the supply of "complex technology" is unlikely to prove an important constraint on its expansion. As we have seen, supply of this input has responded to demands generated in the sector's product market. As market conditions led firms to enter product lines which required advanced know-how, they increased their own engineering staffs to develop internal technical capacity, and, when they wished to, imported know-how from foreign consulting and production firms. Concerning the latter, we noted a series of reasons why foreign companies have been willing to negotiate know-how agreements on terms which the sector's Brazilian firms consider entirely reasonable. Finally, in interviews, the sector's entrepreneurs expressed little concern about the supply of know-how, and they contemplate with equanimity the prospect of future expansion into more technically specialized fields, as indeed they have constantly done in the past.[11]

The ECLA mission that studied this sector and gave special attention to potential difficulties connected with the transmission of "complex technology" reached similar conclusions on this point: "The technical limitations on the possibilities of domestic production are due to the need to employ processes . . . not available to domestic industry and beyond its technological capacity. This second limiting factor is, however, due in most cases almost entirely to the size of the market . . . Current industrial development in Brazil has shown a surprising ability to absorb technological improvements once the length of the production series justifies the effort of adaptation and the investment involved. In other words,

11. The measures temporarily implemented by the Brazilian government in early 1964 in an effort to reduce dependence on foreign know-how and stimulate domestic research and development work would, however, have led to technical and eventual economic stagnation of the industries working with complex technology. The question was approached as a simple case of import substitution, in which when importation is impeded—in this case by forcing the suspension of licensing agreements—local production responds to supply the domestic market. A necessary condition for an elastic production response, however, is elastic supply of required inputs. But one of the principal inputs to the research and development process is specialized technical knowledge and experience, and the Brazilian firms were being denied the possibility of making further gains in this direction by the termination of licensing agreements.

the technological limitation is essentially a limitation caused by the size of the market."[12]

In the previous chapters we have noted the importance of final product demand in generating dynamic supply of factors to the sector. Let us now consider the demand for capital goods in Brazil.

12. ECLA, *Basic Equipment in Brazil*, p. 16; see also p. 63.

V

DEMAND

In turning from the conditions of factor supply to a consideration of market conditions, the focus of our study also changes. Previously we dealt mainly with one sector of the capital goods industry, heavy-engineering products. As mentioned in Chapter I, this restriction was dictated by the availability of data. When we turn to demand conditions, however, the situation on data resources is reversed. Extensive quantitative material could not be obtained from firms of the sector, but was available for the industry as a whole from such sources as the industrial censuses and the national income accounts time-series on capital formation.[1] Consequently, the scope of the study now broadens to include the entire Brazilian capital goods industry.

Let us consider the market for equipment in Brazil: its size, determinants, cyclical conditions, and time trends. Because demand for equipment is closely linked with aggregate investment, this leads to a general discussion of savings and investment in Brazilian development.

SOME CHARACTERISTICS OF THE MARKET

SIZE AND DISTRIBUTION

In the period 1947–1959, gross fixed capital formation in Brazil averaged 15.5 percent and investment in machinery 9.0 percent of gross national product.[2] Data on the distribution of these equipment purchases among client sectors in 1949 and 1958 are presented in Table V–1.

1. Most of the statistical material used in this chapter is from the Fundação Getúlio Vargas of Rio de Janeiro, henceforth referred to as FGV. Estimates of gross investment are available from 1939 to 1960. For the period 1939–1947, these are published in Grupo Misto BNDE-CEPAL, *Análise e Projeções do Desenvolvimento Econômico* (Rio de Janeiro, 1957); for later years, in Ministério de Planejamento, *Programa de Ação Econômica do Govêrno Revolucionario* (Rio de Janeiro, 1964). For the years 1947–1959, the data on gross investment are also available disaggregated into construction, equipment purchases from domestic suppliers and from imports, and inventory changes.
2. Calculated from data supplied by the FGV.

TABLE V-1. Distribution of Equipment Purchases in Brazil, 1949 and 1958 (Percent)

Sector	1949	1958
Agriculture	8.0	9.7
Electricity	9.7	10.9
Transportation	45.8	43.9[a]
Services	13.2	11.8
Manufacturing	23.3	23.7
	100.0	100.0

Source: Ministério de Planejamento, *Programa de Ação Economica do Govêrno Revolucionario* (Rio de Janeiro, 1964).

[a]Another study, cited in "Fifteen Years of Economic Policy in Brazil," *Economic Bulletin for Latin America,* 9 (March 1964), p. 165, Table 3, presents data that suggest that the investment in transportation took a smaller share, approximately 36.2% of gross investment of machinery.

Agriculture's share in total equipment purchases appears relatively low, particularly if we bear in mind that approximately one quarter of Brazilian national product was produced in that sector.[3] The large share of equipment for transportation activities is also noteworthy. Manufacturing industry took approximately 24 percent of all equipment. And, as the table shows, the distribution of equipment purchases by client sector did not change greatly during this period.

CHANGES WITHIN THE AGGREGATE DEMAND FOR EQUIPMENT

There were, however, other important shifts within the market for equipment. First of all, the output mix within manufacturing industry changed, as the metallurgical, chemical, and metal-working industries grew much more rapidly than the industrial sector as a whole. As the data in Table V–2 indicate, the percentage of these industries in total industrial value added increased by about 75 percent between 1949 and 1959. The changed composition

3. The functional categories in Table V-1 may obscure substitution in the type of equipment used. For example, whereas agriculture in some countries may use more machinery in production, under Brazilian conditions of extensive cultivation and a moving frontier, relatively more equipment may be used in transportation of goods which can be grown more economically at greater distances.

TABLE V-2. Percentage of the Metallurgical, Chemical, Mechanical, Electrical, and Transportation-Equipment Industries
in Total Industrial Value Added, 1949 and 1959

Industry	1949	1959
Metallurgical	9.4	11.9
Chemical	5.3	8.7
Mechanical	2.1	3.5
Transportation-equipment	2.2	7.6
Electrical-material	1.6	3.9
	20.6	35.6

Source: Calculated from data in IBGE, *Censo Industrial* (Rio de
Janeiro, 1963).

of the industrial sector's output has meant an increasing relative
importance for producers' goods used in those industries.

Another important change is the vastly expanded participation
of the public sector in aggregate capital formation. This occurred
as the government expanded its investment activity in some
traditional areas, such as road construction; as it took over activities
formerly carried on by foreign companies, for instance, in railroads,
coastal shipping, and electricity; and as it entered new fields, such
as petroleum and steel production. Between 1947–1949 and 1958–
1960, the public sector's share in gross fixed-capital formation more
than doubled, rising from 22 percent to 55 percent of the total.[4] In
the process, some individual public-sector corporations became
major clients in the Brazilian equipment market.[5]

4. These figures were calculated from data on the share in aggregate fixed capital formation of the federal, state, and local governments, published in the national income accounts
issue of *Revista Brasileira de Economia* 16 (March 1962). To these data I have added the figures
on the annual investments by the principal public-sector corporations: the Development
Bank; the Federal Road Department, the Petrobrás, which was kind enough to furnish data
on its investments as of 1955; and the corporation which built Brasília, whose investments are
included as of 1957. Data for this last company's investments are calculated from "Gastos
Públicos em Brasília," *Conjuntura Econômica*, 16 (December 1962). A study by the Brazilian
Planning Ministry gives similar high figures for the share of the public sector in gross fixed
capital formation. See Ministério de Planejamento, EPEA, *O Mercado Brasileiro de Capitais*
(Rio de Janeiro, 1965), pp. 39–40.

5. Disaggregated investment data for all the public-sector corporations are not available,
but we can see the percentage of the equipment purchases of one government corporation, the
petroleum company, in total equipment purchases of these years: 1955, 4.0; 1956, 3.9; 1957,
0.9; 1958, 1.6; 1959, 1.4. (Computed from data kindly supplied by the Economics Division of
the Petrobrás, and from the figures on aggregate equipment purchased, supplied by the
FGV.)

These developments were partly responsible for another important change within the market, an increasing interest in better equipment. According to domestic and foreign capital goods producers, the Brazilian equipment market has frequently been a low-price, low-quality market compared with the developed countries.[6] Equipment purchasers have often preferred to buy cheaper capital goods rather than products of greater quality and longevity.[7] This trait still distinguishes part of the Brazilian market from equipment demand in the advanced countries, but notable changes have apparently occurred since the early 1950's, as an increasing fraction of the market became willing and able to purchase better-quality equipment despite its higher price.

This shift appears to have followed from changes in two key variables affecting investors' choice of equipment: the marginal cost of funds and the pay-out period used in discounting future income streams. Many of the clients for capital goods who established themselves in the 1950's—whether among the Brazilian "economic groups," the local subsidiaries of international corporations, or the public-sector companies—can now make their investment calculations with a reasonably long time-horizon.[8] This investment behavior contrasts with that before the chronic, postwar balance-of-payments crisis shifted relative prices in favor of local production for many products, and gave a firm basis and apparently irreversible policy commitment to Brazilian industrialization. Because of these developments, investors could rationally make their investment plans without the relatively short ("fly-by-night") pay-out period which earlier conditions may have dictated.[9]

6. H. J. Habakkuk, in his *American and British Technology in the Nineteenth Century* (New York, 1962), pp. 56–63, 86–90, cites a similar phenomenon in comparisons of nineteenth-century British and American technology: the Americans often preferred equipment that lacked durability, as compared with British practice in the same industries. He attributes this to various causes, including American biases for rapid change and modernization, greater expectations of rapid technical obsolescence in equipment, and capital shortage. Of these factors, only the last seems relevant in the Brazilian case.

7. The usual implication is that domestic clients preferred cheaper products despite a rising marginal quality/cost ratio which would enable them to get much more durable equipment for only a small unit price increase.

8. The "economic groups" are the large Brazilian enterprises, somewhat similar to the Japanese *zaibatsu*, with strong financial, technical, and political resources and usually with operations in several different industries.

9. Comments on the apparent irrationality and the "short-sightedness" implicit in many local investment calculations during the earlier period—*imediatismo*, as it was called—are common. Cf., e.g., the frequent remarks by Dorival Teixeira Vieira in his lecture notes, "O Desenvolvimento Econômico do Brasil," mimeographed (University of São Paulo, 1962).

Furthermore, many equipment purchasers have been able to make their investment calculations assuming a relatively elastic supply of cheap capital. This is especially true of the public-sector corporations, which have had easy access to the government-controlled Banco do Brasil (the country's largest commercial bank) and to the National Development Bank. To a lesser degree, private firms in high-priority sectors have also had good access to these banks. Moreover, in many of the new industries on which Brazilian industrial expansion has been based, rapidly growing demand and oligopolistic market structure have provided firms with relatively high profits with which to finance their capacity expansion.[10] Again, the contrast is with pre-1945 Brazilian manufacturing, when less favorable demand conditions and relative ease of entry may often have prevented firms from achieving very high rates of return. In the 1950's, however, although there was credit rationing and few firms had "enough" capital, to a much greater degree than before the marginal cost of funds to a firm was not so high that it precluded purchase of better-quality, more expensive equipment. As we will see in the next chapter, domestic equipment producers have responded to these changes within the equipment market, and have greatly improved the quality of their production.

FLUCTUATIONS IN DEMAND

In the advanced countries, demand in the capital goods industries has sometimes been noted for its large cyclical fluctuations. Indeed, fluctuations in capital goods demand have been large enough to generate cycles in aggregate production. By comparison, demand for capital goods in Brazil has grown relatively smoothly. Table V–3 shows the annual changes in total *ex post* demand for equipment during the years 1948–1959. The data are also disaggregated to show the annual changes in equipment

10. Oligopolistic market structure does not guarantee high profits, but this seems often to have occurred in many Brazilian industries during the late 1950's and early 1960's. The following concentration ratios, showing the share of the three largest firms in total industry output (despite a much larger number of firms in the same industry), are available for the early 1960's: agriculture tools, 97%; refrigerators, 86%; washing machines, 82%. Data are from "Auge y Declinación del Proceso de Sustitución de Importaciones in el Brasil," *Boletín Económico de América Latina*, 9 (March 1964), 57. Similarly high concentration also occurs in such industries as petroleum, chemicals, automobiles, steel, and other metallurgical production. These are industries which, as mentioned, account for a relatively large share of Brazilian industrial output, and particularly much of its recent growth.

Table V-3. Annual Percentage Change in Equipment Purchases, 1948–1959

Year	Total purchases	Imports	Domestic supply
1948	9	−4	20
1949	2	−12	9
1950	−3	−17	4
1951	28	53	18
1952	0	0	1
1953	−19	−46	−5
1954	53	82	44
1955	−9	−22	−4
1956	0	−13	4
1957	3	48	−9
1958	9	1	12
1959	25	13	20

Source: Computed from data supplied by the FGV. The deflator used was index 63, "Metallurgical Prices," published in *Conjuntura Econômica.*

purchases from imports and from domestic supply.

Imports fluctuated much more than domestically produced equipment, with twice as high an average annual percentage change. In fact, imports account for most of the cyclical fluctuations observed in the aggregate data of Table V–3. By contrast, demand for domestic equipment products showed few downward movements and a smoother upward trend.

Imports have fluctuated so widely because, as we will see in the next chapter, equipment imports have been highly dependent on the availability of foreign credits. The fluctuations reflect the sharp movements of foreign capital inflow. Capital goods from domestic sources, however, have followed a much steadier upward trend. As discussed below, domestic investment demand has been closely correlated with the level of lagged income, and hence has been sensitive to changes in the rate of growth. Thus the absence of sharp fluctuations in demand for domestic equipment appears to be due to the relative stability of aggregate growth in Brazil during these years.[11] When the export boom of the early postwar years

11. The stability of Brazilian growth in the years 1947–1959 is illustrated by the fact that the standard deviation of the annual growth rate is only 5% higher than the annual average.

ended, import substitution and public-sector investment programs took its place.[12] As a result, the domestic capital goods industry was spared the sharp downward movements characteristic of countries where economic growth has come in a less steady manner.

DETERMINANTS OF MARKET SIZE

In an attempt to analyze the determinants of the size of the market for equipment and investment goods in Brazil, efforts were made to relate observed demand with other relevant macroeconomic variables.[13] Brazilian data, however, do not permit detailed analysis of investment decisions by industry. On the demand side, there are no time series of capacity utilization that, through an accelerator process, might determine the demand for capital goods. On the side of resources for financing investment, there are no reliable sectoral data on profits, corporate reserves, or other forms of liquidity which might be used to test a residual-funds hypothesis. Some of these problems also apply at the macro level and preclude a sophisticated approach to aggregate investment. Reliable investment estimates are too recent to permit a long time series of aggregate capital stock that might be used for testing a Kaldor-type demand relation for investment goods. There also are no estimates of savings distinct from those of actual *ex post* investment. Because of these limitations, we cannot discuss Brazilian investment behavior, either aggregate or sectoral, in terms as refined as those found in some studies in the developed countries.[14]

12. The only exceptions to this pattern of steady growth occurred in 1953 and 1956. In both cases this apparently resulted from the decline in export receipts and of imports in the preceding years, and the tight money policies which were implemented in an effort to deal with the ensuing acceleration of the inflation.

13. In this chapter we will confine ourselves to domestic demand for capital goods. Although the price and quality of Brazilian capital goods often meet world market competition, and some export sales have taken place, the export market has been hampered for several reasons. First, the export exchange-rate has usually been overvalued. Secondly, many firms in the capital goods industry are either subsidiaries of foreign firms or work under licensing agreements from overseas companies. In both cases, the foreign firms have preferred to have their home-country and third-country markets serviced directly from their home-country plants. Finally, export sales have been severely hampered by lack of suppliers' credits, which are a very important aspect of international competition in these product markets.

14. See, for example, L. R. Klein and A. S. Goldberger, *An Econometric Model of the United States, 1929–1952* (Amsterdam, 1955); J. R. Meyer and Edwin Kuh, *The Investment Decision* (Cambridge, Mass., 1957); and J. R. Meyer and R. R. Glauber, *Investment Decisions, Economic Forecasting, and Public Policy* (Boston, 1964).

On theoretical grounds, however, one might expect that the determinants of investment in Brazil during the years 1947–1959 (the period for which data on equipment purchases are available) might be simpler than in an advanced country; and thus we might arrive at significant relationships even with the limited data available. Specifically, on a priori grounds, there are reasons for expecting that the level of real investment was governed by factors on the supply side, from the flow of savings to finance capital formation. Under the conditions of inflation and rapidly growing aggregate demand which characterized Brazil during most of these years, investors had probably not adjusted actual with desired capital stock. Indeed, throughout this period there is abundant testimony from bankers and investors on unsatisfied demand for investment credits, and capital rationing slowed many private and public investment projects. Moreover, investors have always drawn to the maximum upon the equipment credits available from foreign suppliers. Therefore the flow of real savings to finance equipment purchases would appear to be the relevant constraint on capital goods demand. Because during most of the period 1947–1959 the Brazilian economy was probably producing at ceiling levels, a neoclassical rather than a Keynesian model is suggested, in which savings determine investment rather than vice cersa.

With these considerations in mind, an effort was made to fit regression equations with the supply of savings as the independent variable and investment as the dependent variable. As mentioned above, however, there are no Brazilian estimates of savings independent of actual *ex post* investment. As a substitute, the level of income in the previous year (Y_{t-1}) was used, in which, as we will see, there seems to be a fairly stable savings relation. To this was added, as a second source of resources to finance capital formation, annual net foreign-capital inflow, $NFCI_t$. Using these independent variables and taking gross equipment purchases, GEQ_t, as the dependent variable, a function was fitted by least squares. Thirteen observations, expressed in billions of 1949 cruzeiros, were available.[15] The estimated regression equation is

(1.1) $\quad GEQ_t = 0.093\,(Y_{t-1}) + 0.334\,NFCI_t.$

15. Data were kindly supplied by the FGV. The deflator used was the implicit GNP price deflator. In this and in the other equations reported below, the intercept was eliminated when it was not statistically different from zero.

The corrected R^2 is 0.793, and the F-ratio for the equation is significant above the 1-percent level. The t-test for the regression coefficients is significant at the 1-percent and 10-percent levels, respectively. The Durbin-Watson statistic is 2.257.

A separate equation was also estimated for the gross equipment supplied by domestic producers, 1947–1959:

$$(1.2) \quad GEQ_{\text{dom}} = -5.759 + 0.091\ (Y_{t-1}).$$

The corrected R^2 is 0.874. The F-ratio is significant at the 1-percent level, and t-test for the intercept and for regression weight is significant at the 5-percent level. The Durbin-Watson statistic is 2.125.

The relatively good fit of these equations and the high level of statistical significance of the regression weights on lagged income seem to be part of a general pattern of investment in Brazil. Taking gross investment (GI_t)—that is, gross fixed capital formation plus changes in inventories—as the dependent variable, other functions were fitted, this time using the 21 observations available from 1940 to 1960.[16] Gross investment was regressed against lagged income and current foreign-capital inflow; and in an accelerator-type relation, against the first difference of current and previous income. The estimated equations are:

$$(2.1) \quad GI_t = 0.165\ (Y_{t-1}) + 0.849\ NFCI_t;$$
corrected $R^2 = 0.899$; Durbin-Watson statistic $= 1.975$.

$$(2.2.1) \quad 1940–1960: \quad GI_t = 16.768 + 1.615\ (Y_t - Y_{t-1});$$
corrected $R^2 = 0.451$; Durbin-Watson statistic $= 1.125$.

$$(2.2.2) \quad 1947–1960: \quad GI_t = 10.213 + 1.785\ (Y_t - Y_{t-1});$$
corrected $R^2 = 0.876$; Durbin-Watson statistic $= 1.314$.

In all cases, the F-ratio for the equation is significant above the 1-percent level, the t-test for the regression weights above the 5-percent level.

These equations clearly present some problems in interpretation. There is an identification problem in distinguishing whether they relate to savings or to investment behavior, though, as mentioned earlier, on theoretical grounds we would expect Brazilian invest-

16. For the years 1947–1960, data were available from FGV. For the years 1939–1947, data are from Grupo Misto BNDE-CEPAL *Análise e Projeções*, Statistical Appendix, Tables 1, 5, 9, 10.

ment to have been determined by savings during this period. There is also the problem of strong time trends in the series for investment and national income. Because of the stability of Brazilian development during this period, the trend correlation between these variables is also the essence of the causal relationship: that is, that savings and investment increased steadily to permit continuing aggregate growth. Indeed, what is perhaps most interesting about the relatively good fit of these equations is the stability they indicate for Brazilian investment during these years.[17] During the period 1940–1960, there were several important political crises and uncertainty concerning other possible shifts. Varying restrictions were placed on imports; there were several exchange-rate devaluations and policy changes in the direction of tight money. Throughout the period internal inflation continued, but with variable rates which prevented accurate forecasting and prior adjustment. Despite the risks and uncertainties that these conditions added to investment decision-making, Brazilian investment appears as a stable function rather than an erratic variable responding to random disturbances.

Finally, we should note that aggregate domestic savings in Brazil have been relatively high by comparison with other underdeveloped countries. In a cross-section study of 34 countries, Charles Wolf, Jr. accounted for 84 percent of the variance in per capita savings with a model which took the level of per capita income and foreign trade as the exogenous variables.[18] In 1955–1960, Brazil's per capita savings were 20 percent higher than predicted by the model.

ALLOCATION OF GROSS INVESTMENT TO USES OTHER THAN EQUIPMENT

We can also discuss the size of the market for equipment in terms of the other claimants on gross investment and their time trends.[19] In the years 1947–1960, for which disaggregated investment data are available, inventories averaged 8 percent of gross

---

17. A simultaneous-equations model has also indicated a stable investment function for Brazil. See H. S. Odeh, *The Impact of Inflation on the Level of Economic Activity* (Rotterdam, 1964), chap. VII, esp. pp. 81–91.

18. Charles Wolf, Jr., "Savings Regressions, 'Self-Help' and Development Performance," mimeographed (Santa Monica: The RAND Corporation, 1964), pp. 18–21.

19. The question of time trends of the share of gross investment itself in GNP is discussed in a subsequent section.

investment. Excluding the early postwar years when the large coffee stocks that accumulated during World War II were sold off, inventories took approximately 15 percent of all investment. Toward the end of this period and into the early 1960's, inventories rose sharply as the government bought coffee stocks in an effort to maintain the world coffee-price.[20] Because of this development, there was no tendency for inventories to decline as a percentage of gross investment.

Disaggregating further the market for investment goods, we find that equipment accounted for approximately 60 percent of expenditure on gross fixed capital formation. In current prices, this share tended to increase slightly during this period.[21] Deducting expenditure on construction from gross fixed capital formation, we have the percentage of equipment purchases in gross national product. This came to approximately 9 percent during these years, with no upward or downward trend.[22] In absolute figures, this market amounted to some 1,400 million dollars in 1950–1954 and 2,000 million dollars in 1955–1961.[23]

SAVINGS AND INVESTMENT OVER TIME

Aggregate Brazilian savings were adequate to finance almost 95 percent of the gross investment necessary for the country's rapid

20. We see below data on additions to government coffee-stock purchases as a percentage of Brazilian GNP during the years 1957–1962:

1957	1.1%	1960	2.1%
1958	2.1%	1961	0.9%
1959	2.8%	1962	2.0%

(Data are from "Fifteen Years of Economic Policy in Brazil," *Economic Bulletin for Latin America*, 9 (November 1964), 183). Thus in some years, government coffee accumulation amounted to more than 10% of gross Brazilian investment.

21. This was computed from data supplied by FGV. In constant (1949) prices, however, the share of equipment in gross fixed capital formation may have fallen somewhat between 1947–1948 and 1957–1959. In computing Brazilian fixed capital formation at constant prices, the deflator used for construction was the *Conjuntura Econômica* index of construction costs in Rio de Janeiro. (The movements of this index were closely paralleled in a series for construction costs in São Paulo: "Indice do Custo de Construção para O Estado de São Paulo," put together and kindly made available by the firm of Hoffman Bosworth do Brasil.) The deflator for domestically produced equipment was *Conjuntura Econômica* index 63; and the deflator for imported equipment was constructed from data supplied by SUMOC on the *câmbio de custo* exchange-rate, under which most equipment was imported during this period.

22. Calculated from data supplied by the FGV. Table V-6 of the Statistical Appendix to this chapter presents the annual data in tabular form.

23. Computed from data in *The Economic Development of Latin America in the Post-War Period* (New York: United Nations, 1964), p. 113.

rate of development, and did increase *pari passu* with national income. However, the proportion of GNP allocated to savings and investment showed no tendency to rise in the 22 years, 1939–1960, for which official data are available. Table V–4 presents the gross investment and the domestic savings coefficients for those years. Equations fitted to these series showed no statistically significant trend.

Similarly, in the period 1947–1959 (for which disaggregated investment data were available), gross fixed capital formation in

TABLE V-4. Gross Investment and Gross Domestic Savings as Percentages of Brazilian GNP, 1939–1960

Year	Gross investment coefficient	3-year moving average	Gross domestic savings coefficient	3-year moving average
1939	16.0	—	17.3	—
1940	15.0	15.4	15.4	16.7
1941	15.1	15.1	17.4	17.3
1942	15.2	15.7	19.3	19.0
1943	16.7	16.5	20.6	20.3
1944	16.7	16.1	21.1	19.9
1945	14.0	15.9	18.0	19.4
1946	16.0	15.2	19.1	16.0
1947	15.7	15.8	13.8	16.4
1948	15.8	14.9	16.4	14.4
1949	13.2	13.5	13.1	13.7
1950	11.5	14.6	11.6	13.6
1951	19.0	17.0	16.1	14.8
1952	20.4	17.7	16.6	15.5
1953	13.8	18.3	13.8	17.0
1954	20.7	17.0	20.6	16.9
1955	16.4	17.4	16.3	17.4
1956	15.2	15.9	15.3	15.5
1957	16.2	15.8	14.8	14.0
1958	15.9	17.4	14.5	15.8
1959	20.0	17.9	18.1	16.0
1960	17.9	—	15.4	—

Sources: Data for the years 1939–1946 are from CEPAL-BNDE, *Análise e Projeções do Desenvolvimento Econômico* (Rio de Janeiro, 1956); for subsequent years from *Revista Brasileira de Economia*, 16 (March 1962). Gross domestic savings were obtained by deducting net foreign capital inflow from gross investment.

constant prices showed no tendency to rise as a proportion of national income.[24] Estimates of Brazilian national income and savings going back to the 1920's and 1930's indicate that, if anything, aggregate savings rates have *declined* somewhat in the course of the development process.[25]

Before discussing the absence of an upward trend in the domestic-savings coefficient, we should consider the reliability of the savings and investment data. In the Brazilian national income accounts, the estimates of saving are derived from data on the supply of investment goods. Thus components of savings which might be missed because of under-reporting or data collection problems (for example, saving and investment by un-incorporated firms) do, in fact, enter the figures. Statistics for imported producers' goods are readily available. For domestic supply, the estimates are derived from the output of the cement, metallurgical, and mechanical industries. The collection of these production figures from a few key industries does not present a great problem, and the procedure takes note of the investment goods purchased by demand components which might be missed by other collection methods. Hence the data on capital formation appear to be reasonably reliable. These considerations relate to the *level* of the savings and investment ratios; but in any case, there seems no reason to posit a systematic *trend* leading to a downward bias over time in the estimation of the aggregate investment and savings coefficients.

THE BRAZILIAN EXPERIENCE AND SOME THEORIES OF SAVING AND INVESTMENT IN UNDERDEVELOPED COUNTRIES

The absence of an upward trend in the savings and investment ratios has not always been noted in analysis of Brazilian development. And, as mentioned in Chapter II, the capital goods industry and the government planning authority also assumed that demand for investment goods would increase more than proportionally with national income. More generally, the Brazilian experience does not conform to some models of savings and investment in underdeveloped countries, according to which the marginal savings rate

24. See Table V-7 in the Statistical Appendix to this chapter.
25. Octávio Dias Carneiro, "Past Trends of Structural Relationships in the Economic Evolution of Brazil, 1920–1965," mimeographed (Cambridge, Mass.: Center for International Affairs, Harvard University, 1966), pp. 17–18 and Tables IXB and XXIXA.

might be expected to exceed the average, and raise the latter in the process of development. The income-elasticity of savings supply is clearly of major interest, for most macro analytical and planning models depend heavily on assumptions concerning the marginal savings rate. Despite the importance of the subject, relatively little empirical evidence has been brought to bear on the theories advanced in the literature on economic development. Brazil is particularly useful for a case study, because some of these are "vicious circle" theories that attempt to explain why a less-developed country which has never experienced economic growth does not increase the fraction of its income that it saves and invests. Brazil, however, has had rapid and sustained growth, as well as many other developments whose absence is claimed to impede savings and investment in underdeveloped countries.

To deal first with factors on the supply side, it has been suggested that while the price-elasticity of savings may be low in under-developed countries, the income-elasticity should be relatively high.[26] That is, rising levels of income may themselves be enough to increase savings rates, by enabling an underdeveloped country to break out of the vicious circle: poverty—low savings—low invest-ment—poverty. This suggestion is supported by the general observation that savings rates are often higher in rich countries than in poor ones.[27] The argument gains further a priori appeal when placed in the framework of a model such as W. A. Lewis'

26. Paul N. Rosenstein-Rodan, "Notes on the Theory of the 'Big Push,'" in *Economic Development for Latin America*, ed. H. S. Ellis (London, 1961), p. 65. Cf. also Harvey Leiben-stein, *Economic Backwardness and Economic Growth* (New York, 1960), pp. 197–199.

27. Cf., e.g., Simon Kuznets, "Quantitative Aspects of the Growth of Nations: Share and Structure of Consumption," *Economic Development and Cultural Change*, 10 (October 1961), 5, 21, and Appendix Table I. Actually, the evidence on the subject is not completely conclusive. H. S. Houthakker, in a study using the national income statistics for 34 countries during the 1950's, found some evidence of slight curvilinearity between aggregate domestic savings and national income. See his "On Some Determinants of Savings in Developed and Under-Developed Countries," in *Problems of Economic Development*, ed. E. A. G. Robinson (London, 1965), pp. 220–221. Charles Wolf, Jr., has also obtained statistically significant correlations between per capita domestic savings and national income in cross-section analysis of 34 underdeveloped countries. See his "Savings Regressions." I computed a rank-order correla-tion between per capita income and the gross investment coefficient in 64 countries. The Spearman coefficient obtained is 0.645, significant at the 1% level. (The data used were from Bruce Russett et al., *World Handbook of Political and Social Indicators* [New Haven, 1964]. Countries which have had a large volume of foreign capital inflow—e.g., Algeria, Israel, Canada, Puerto Rico, Taiwan, Panama, South Korea, and Rhodesia—were excluded.) Such cross-section analysis does not, of course, necessarily imply that within a *single* country, savings rates will increase as income rises.

"Economic Development with Unlimited Supplies of Labour."[28] Under conditions of elastic labor supply at constant, low real wages, profits in the capitalistic sector are high. Because the entrepreneur is assumed to have an above-average marginal propensity to save and invest, much of this "surplus" is reinvested. In this process, the capitalist sector expands, raising with it the aggregate savings and investment coefficients.

During this period, developments approximating these conditions occurred in Brazil. The rate of growth of income accelerated from annual figures of 3–4 percent in the 1920's and 1930's to 5–6 percent in the postwar period;[29] and real income increased approximately 139 percent between 1939 and 1960.[30] Per capita income also rose, at a cumulative annual rate of 2.4 percent. Moreover, although real wages sometimes also increased, they generally rose less than worker productivity, so that in dynamic terms the Lewis model was approximated.[31]

Reflecting these developments, the "modern" sector did expand considerably. Between 1947–1949 and 1958–1960, the share of corporate depreciation allowances and retained profits in GNP

28. In *The Manchester School*, 24 (May 1954); reprinted in *The Economics of Underdevelopment*, ed. A. N. Agarwala and S. P. Singh (Bombay, 1961), pp. 400–449.

29. See Houthakker, "On Some Determinants," p. 222, for evidence on the role of the rate of income growth in determining aggregate savings ratios. Data on growth rates in the 1920's and 1930's are from Carneiro, "Past Trends of Structural Relationships," Table IC.

30. Any calculation of the progress of real wages during this period depends crucially on the choice of years selected, in terms of the dates in which the minimum wage rate was adjusted. It appears, however, that through most of the 1950's some increase in real wages did occur. This was generally less than the increase in worker productivity, however, as the following table, calculated from 1949 and 1959 figures in the *Censo Industrial*, indicates.

Percentage increase per worker, 1949–1959

Industry	Real Wages	Value Added
All manufacturing	26	57
Metallurgical	13	15
Electrical equipment	11	9
Mechanical	7	10
Transportation equipment	−4	14
Textiles	21	30
Leather products	18	33

The following procedures were used in making these computations. In deflating wages, the São Paulo cost-of-living index was used, because the great majority of the Brazilian industrial work-force is concentrated in that area. In deflating the value added per worker, the relevant industry price index, published in *Conjuntura Econômica*, was used.

31. Data in this paragraph are from FGV. The increase in real income is calculated in constant prices of 1949. Data for 1939–1947 are from Grupo Misto BNDE-CEPAL, *Análise e Projeções*.

increased approximately 50 percent.[32] This amounted to a net increase in the investment resources available to the corporate sector, for this period saw virtually no decline in the percentage of investment funds coming from sources external to the firm.[33] Despite these developments, the aggregate savings coefficient did not rise.[34]

The public sector also increased the share of its expenditure in GNP sharply, approximately 70 percent between 1947–1949 and 1958–1960,[35] and public-sector investments increased proportionately with the public sector's share in GNP.[36]

Several important policy measures were also undertaken in an effort to promote increased domestic savings and investment. The government cheapened the relative price of producers' equipment to potential investors by permitting duty-free importation of equipment in a period when the tariffs on most other imports rose steeply.[37] In addition, foreign exchange for servicing debts incurred with overseas machinery-suppliers was also available under subsidized terms. Measures were also taken to overcome the capital-market imperfections, such as the unavailability of long-term investment funds, that were believed to have inhibited

32. See Table V-8 in the Statistical Appendix to this chapter. Some writers have suggested that the Brazilian inflation transferred resources from wage earners to entrepreneurs and "the producer sector." The evidence for such reallocation effects is not at all conclusive, however. In any case, since the aggregate savings and investment coefficients did not rise, such a process would imply a transfer from wage earners' consumption to entrepreneurs' consumption.

33. See Werner Baer, "Brazil: Inflation and Economic Efficiency," *Economic Development and Cultural Change*, 11 (July 1963), Table 3.

34. In a discussion of an apparently similar case, that of Mexico in the 1940's and early 1950's, Adolph Sturmthal suggests that the entrepreneurs' marginal propensity to save may be lower than their average. See his "Economic Development, Income Distribution, and Capital Formation in Mexico," *Journal of Political Economy*, 63 (June 1955), 195.

35. See W. A. Lewis, *The Theory of Economic Growth* (Homewood, Ill., 1955), pp. 225 ff., for the suggestion that such a development might raise marginal savings and investment rates. The public sector's expenditure share was computed from data on the federal, state, and local governments and the major public-sector corporations, data kindly made available by Dr. Margaret Hanson Costa, Center for Fiscal Studies, FGV. Annual data are presented in Table V-9. These data relate to public-sector expenditure; but the Brazilian public sector's tax revenues also rose sharply, from 15% of GNP in 1947–1949 to 23% in 1958–1960. As a result of this development, the Brazilian public-sector's revenue share has been unusually high in comparison with other underdeveloped countries. See, for example, H. H. Hinrichs, "Determinants of Government Revenue Shares in Less-Developed Countries," *Economic Journal*, 75 (September 1965).

36. See the annual data presented in Table V-10.

37. In the middle and late 1950's, tariff legislation was applied to many types of equipment. In practice, however, duty-free importation continued, for other legislation and administrative rulings in the National Tariff Council created a very long list of exemptions to the tariff code. This is discussed in Chap. VI.

Brazilians from saving and investing in nontraditional activities or industries of high capital-intensity and large minimum scale. The government founded "mixed enterprises" in industries such as steel, petroleum, electricity, and transportation. A Development Bank was established which provided long-term capital to the private sector, and which, together with the government-controlled Banco do Brasil, facilitated entry into many new activities.

Apart from these developments on the supply side, the Brazilian experience also presents a contrast with another model that relates the low savings of underdeveloped countries to deficiencies in the *demand* for investment. For example, Hirschman and others have argued that the decision to save in an underdeveloped country is closely conditioned by the decision to invest. The latter, however, is constrained by the limited "ability to invest"; because of a persistent low-income equilibrium, potential entrepreneurs lack experience and capabilities in investing and economic innovation, and are adverse to its uncertainties.[38] Over the past decades in Brazil, however, potential investors have seen that entrepreneurs undertaking investments have generally been rewarded by the economy's continuing high growth, and aversion to innovating behavior should have declined. And, as a result of the experience and learning generated by Brazil's sustained growth, the "ability to invest" should have increased, raising savings rates with it.

BRAZILIAN SAVINGS AND FOREIGN INVESTMENT

Not only did these domestic developments fail to raise Brazilian investment and savings rates, but this period also saw a sharp change in the situation regarding foreign investment. In earlier years net foreign-capital movements had sometimes been negative and a drain on savings resources. In the 1950's, however, the flow was reversed with, in some years, substantial net inflow of foreign capital, in the form of commercial credits mainly, and, to a lesser extent, direct foreign investment.

The fact that this increase in the supply of capital was not associated with a rise in the investment and savings coefficients is

38. Cf. Albert O. Hirschman, *The Strategy of Economic Development* (New Haven, 1963), pp. 33–49; Leibenstein, *Economic Backwardness*, chap. 9, esp. pp. 125–135; and Henry C. Aubrey, "Investment Decisions in Underdeveloped Countries," in *Capital Formation and Economic Growth*, National Bureau of Economic Research (Princeton, 1955), esp. pp. 404–415.

surprising. It might be expected that in an economy with a per capita income of 200–300 dollars, and with demand growing as rapidly as in Brazil, the range of untapped investment opportunities and demand for investment funds would be so great that an increase in capital supplied from abroad would mean a net addition to investment resources. Increased foreign investment should therefore have raised the aggregate investment coefficient. The argument might run even more forcefully: that increased foreign investment should also lead to higher *domestic* savings rates. This would occur if foreign capital operated as autonomous investment, opening new industries and generating induced domestic savings and investment. In this perspective, foreign and domestic capital would be complementary rather than competitive in their supply; and indeed much of the discussion of the role of foreign capital in economic development has stressed its effect in promoting internal savings and investment.[39]

In an effort to examine the validity of these arguments in the Brazilian experience, regression equations were fitted in which domestic savings (DS_t) were taken to be determined by the previous year's income (Y_{t-1}) and by net foreign capital inflow in the current year $(NFCI_t)$. Expressed in billions of 1949 cruzeiros, the estimated equation for the 1940–1960 period is

$$(3.1.1) \quad DS_t = 0.155 \ (Y_{t-1}) - 0.156 \ NFCI_t.$$

The corrected R^2 is 0.839, and the F-ratio for the equation is significant above the 1-percent level. The t-test for the regression weights is significant at the 5-percent and 30-percent levels, respectively. The Durbin-Watson statistic is 2.062.

The negative sign of the foreign investment term indicates that during this period foreign investment and domestic saving were inversely related.[40] Excluding the years of World War II and its

39. See, e.g., Hirschman, *Strategy of Economic Development*, pp. 38–39, 206–207. Similarly, John Fei and Douglas Paauw in their discussion of the relation between foreign capital inflow and aggregate growth in underdeveloped countries ("Foreign Assistance and Self-Help," *Review of Economics and Statistics*, 47 [August 1965]), assume as a matter of course that domestic savings and foreign investment will not be inversely related.

40. In his study covering the period 1920–1965 ("Past Trends of Structural Relationships"), Carneiro also remarks on the fact that domestic savings rates declined in the period in which foreign investment increased notably. Cross-section analysis of savings rates in 34 underdeveloped countries by Charles Wolf suggests that in other countries, too, foreign investment may be associated with reduced domestic savings. Of the four countries which Wolf's regression analysis singles out as significantly low savers (Chile, Panama, Puerto Rico, and Algeria), all had had relatively large inflows of foreign capital. See Wolf, "Savings Regressions," esp. pp. 20–24. Another study by Hollis B. Chenery and Peter Eckstein

aftermath and running the regression again gave the following result for the period 1947–1960:

$$(3.1.2) \quad DS_t = .159 \ (Y_{t-1}) + 0.594 \ NFCI_t.$$

The corrected R^2 is 0.822. The F-ratio for the equation is significant above the 1-percent level, and the t-test for the regression weights at the 5-percent and 10-percent levels, respectively. The Durbin-Watson statistic is 2.928.

In this case, the sign of the foreign investment term indicates a direct relation, albeit one which was not strong enough to raise the marginal savings rate. The catalytic effects of foreign capital in inducing a total volume of investment greater than itself are not, however, borne out. That would imply a regression coefficient on the foreign-capital term greater than unity, but in regression equation (2.1) above, the weight is less than one.

CAUSES OF THE UNIT INCOME-ELASTICITY OF SAVINGS

Why, then, despite these developments affecting both the supply and the demand for savings, did the Brazilian marginal savings rate fail to rise in the course of rapid economic development and, indeed, may have declined from the rates achieved in the 1920's and 1930's? Several suggestions can be offered.[41]

First, on the supply side, it would be unrealistic to expect consumption not to have increased at least proportionately with income. Brazilian development has taken place under conditions different from a model in which all increments to income go to an upper class whose marginal propensity to consume is below its average, and whose resistance to "demonstration effects" keeps it so in the course of development.[42] There is no reason to assume that, in a period of rapid social change and introduction of many

indicates that for most Latin American countries in the late 1950's, domestic savings and foreign capital inflow were inversely related. See their "Development Alternatives for Latin America," mimeographed 1966), Table A-5.

41. The net effects of Brazil's persistent inflation on aggregate savings are hard to assess. Inflation doubtless reduced the savings of people who did not have access to direct investment opportunities; but in a period of rapidly expanding demand and pressure on capacity, there is no reason to assume that the inflation caused potential private investors in the corporate and noncorporate sectors to reduce their savings and investment. H. S. Odeh's econometric study of the Brazilian inflation, *The Impact of Inflation*, in fact shows a positive relation between the rate of price increase and the rate of investment.

42. This is the model Veblen used in his interpretation of rising savings rates in nineteenth-century Germany, *Imperial Germany and the Industrial Revolution* (New York, 1915).

new consumer products, the marginal propensity to consume of the Brazilian upper classes did not shift upwards.

Moreover, there appear to have been changes in the distribution of income, as a greater than proportionate part of Brazil's growing GNP has gone to people below the upper stratum. The industrial labor force has been recruited at earnings substantially above those of the agricultural sector. In recent years, even unskilled industrial workers have had wages approximately twice as high as wages in agriculture.[43] As noted above, real wages in the industrial sector have been rising; and Celso Furtado has estimated

TABLE V-5. Socio-Economic Class Distribution in Brazil, Selected Years (Percent)

Class .	1920	1950	1955
Upper and upper-middle	3.5	5.0	6.0
Lower-middle and upper-lower	26.5	45.0	52.0
Lower-lower	70.0	50.0	42.0
	100.0	100.0	100.0

Source: These figures were computed from material in Robert Havighurst and J. Roberto Moreira, *Society and Education in Brazil* (Pittsburgh, 1965), p. 99. Their data, in turn was calculated from the 1920 and 1950 Census of Occupations, and 1955 data from the Brazilian Social Security Institute.

that real wages of agricultural workers also increased.[44] Table V–5 gives some rough data on the extent to which Brazilian development has been accompanied by the movement of part of the population into higher positions, although their income levels are perhaps still too low for them to have much taste for saving or access to real investment opportunities. As we see, the percentage of the population in the lowest stratum has declined markedly in the modern period. If Brazilian development had not taken this course of distributing part of the additional income generated, but had maintained per capita consumption at 1947 levels and allocated the rest of marginal income to savings, then gross investment

43. W. M. Nicholls and R. R. Paiva, "Structure and Productivity of Brazilian Agriculture," mimeographed (Vanderbilt University, 1964), pp. 9, 51, 53.

44. Presidência da Republica, *Plano Trienal de Desenvolvimento Econômico e Social* (Rio de Janeiro, 1962), pp. 26–27.

in 1960 could have been more than twice as high as it actually was.[45]

Furthermore, on the demand side, if savings were conditioned by investment needs, savings rates may have held level because the marginal capital-output ratio did not rise.[46] Hence, time-preferences between present and future income could be satisfied without rising savings rates. First, the relative price of investment goods did not rise, so that higher savings coefficients were not necessary merely to maintain constant rates of real investment. The relative price of equipment did not increase, while the relative price of construction appears to have declined slightly.[47] In both respects, the Brazilian economy avoided the experience of postwar Argentina, which had so large an increase in the relative price of investment goods that the aggregate savings coefficient rose 50 percent in current prices simply to maintain previous rates of real investment.[48]

At the same time, the marginal capital-output ratio showed no tendency to rise despite changes in the composition of investment in the direction of some sectors—for example, roads, steel, and petroleum—with relatively high capital requirements. This was perhaps a consequence of external economies provided by growth in the size of the market and movement along the aggregate production function. This point, however, has been neglected in some discussions of Brazilian development that have assumed that entry into *sectors* of higher capital intensity entailed a rise in the

45. This is the result of calculating gross consumption for the 1960 population at 1947 per capita consumption levels, and subtracting it from 1960 GNP. Cumulative effects on income and savings coming from higher investment levels in the intervening years are not included. Data for this computation are from Banco Nacional de Desenvolvimento Econômico, *XII Exposição sôbre o Programma de Reaparelhamento Econômico* (Rio de Janeiro, 1964), chap. 1, tables III, VI, VII.

46. The Brazilian National Development Bank has estimated the marginal capital-output ratio in Brazil in the period 1947–1960 at approximately 2.1, with no upward trend. See Banco Nacional, *XII Exposição*, chap. 1, tables IX, XI.

47. Data on the relative price of construction are presented in Table V-11. The relative price of equipment is discussed in Chaps. VII and VIII below.

48. The sharp increase in the relative price of investment goods in postwar Argentina was first stressed by R. Hayn in "Capital Formation and Argentina's Price-Cost Structure," *Review of Economics and Statistics*, 44 (November 1962). Subsequent work by Carlos Diaz-Alejandro, "Relative Prices and Capital Formation in Argentina" (mimeographed [Yale University Economic Growth Center, 1965]), disaggregated the total investment-goods price movement and showed that it came from an increase in the relative cost of construction and in the domestic cost of imported equipment, which, because of delays in import substitution, supplied a much larger share of demand for equipment in Brazil.

aggregate capital-output ratio, and the investment needs for a given growth rate.[49] Since the aggregate capital-output ratio did not, in fact, rise, the Brazilian economy could achieve constant rates of growth without higher rates of saving.[50]

In its behavior Brazil seems to approximate a model suggested by Leontief and others, in which the rate of saving and investment is determined by social time-preference and the marginal efficiency of capital.[51] By changing the initial capital endowment, an inflow of foreign capital may result in a reduction of domestic savings. Similarly, an increase in the marginal efficiency of capital, with social time-preference unchanged, may cause a decline in savings and investment. Something of this sort seems to have occurred in Brazil; for neither the increase in foreign investment nor the internal developments affecting the marginal efficiency of capital caused an increase in the share of national income allocated to investment. There is no indication that Brazil was committed to Soviet values, putting the highest priority on maximizing capital formation and growth; and time-preferences were apparently satisfied by the relatively high rate of income growth that was in fact achieved.[52]

49. See, e.g., ECLA, "Auge y Declinación," pp. 59–60.

50. Another factor here may have been a shift within the composition of aggregate investment in construction. The share of nonresidential construction increased, while the percentage of investment in housing, with its lower contribution to output, has declined relatively since World War II and the early postwar years. Direct estimates of the percentage shares of residential and nonresidential construction are not available. Data on the evolution of the two individual components, however, indicate that nonresidential construction has grown much more rapidly. At the same time, the share of all construction within gross fixed capital formation did not increase. Table V-12 presents indices of residential and nonresidential construction, 1944–1960.

51. Wassily Leontief, "Theoretical Note on Time Preference, Productivity of Capital, Stagnation, and Economic Growth," *American Economic Review*, 47 (September 1958). The Leontief conditions for rising savings rates are discussed in greater detail in section III of Nathaniel H. Leff, "Marginal Savings Rates in the Development Process: The Brazilian Experience," *Economic Journal*, 1968.

52. The case of electricity allocations gives some additional insight into Brazilian preference patterns. Between 1953 and 1961, electricity generation in São Paulo State increased at an annual cumulative rate of 10.6%. (Data for this and subsequent statements here are from *Plano de Desehvolvimento Integrado* [São Paulo, 1964], p. 277.) Nevertheless, power shortages continued to hamper industrial expansion, for of the increment to power supply, only 60% went for industrial use, and the rest went for consumption purposes. Although this percentage is "large," it was not enough to prevent severe bottlenecks: when industrial demand pressed upon electricity-supply capacity, the authorities chose to restrict industrial output rather than impose rationing on domestic consumption. This case of unwillingness to sacrifice more from consumption for production purposes occurred, moreover, in São Paulo, generally considered the most "capitalistically" motivated region in Brazil.

SUMMARY AND CONCLUSIONS

Gross fixed-capital formation in Brazil averaged 16 percent of GNP during these years, and the market for equipment was approximately 9 percent. Within the market for investment goods, there were some important shifts, notably in the changed composition of demand for investment goods by industry and the greatly increased role of the public sector in fixed capital formation. The Brazilian market also turned increasingly toward higher-quality equipment, following changed conditions affecting the discount rate and pay-out period used in investment calculations. We also noted the relative absence of sharp cyclical fluctuations in the market for domestically produced equipment during the period 1948–1959. Variations in the total demand for equipment were accounted for largely by movements in imports, resulting from shifts in the availability of foreign credits.

The supply of real savings to finance capital formation seems to have been the major determinant of the demand for investment goods during these years of persistent boom. Contrary to what might have been expected from some models of savings and investment in underdeveloped countries, the aggregate savings and investment ratios showed no upward trend. This behavior of Brazilian savings and investment over time implies that aggregate demand for investment goods cannot be expected to grow more rapidly than GNP. During this period, however, demand for domestic capital goods did increase more rapidly than aggregate demand, for the domestic industry expanded its share in the total market. Following the tables which complete this chapter, we turn to that development.

STATISTICAL APPENDIX

TABLE V-6. Equipment Purchases as a Percentage of
Brazilian GNP, 1947–1959

Year	Percent	3-year moving average
1947	9.2	—
1948	9.3	9.0
1949	8.5	8.5
1950	7.6	8.7
1951	9.9	9.1
1952	9.7	9.0
1953	7.4	9.0
1954	10.0	8.7
1955	8.8	9.4
1956	9.4	8.9
1957	8.5	8.8
1958	8.6	9.0
1959	9.9	—

Source: Computed from data supplied by FGV.

TABLE V-7. Gross Fixed-Capital Formation as a Percentage of GNP, 1947–1959

Year	Fixed investment coefficient (current prices)	3-year moving average	Fixed investment coefficient (1949 prices)	3-year moving average
1947	17.3	—	16.9	—
1948	16.1	16.1	15.0	15.6
1949	15.0	13.9	15.0	14.7
1950	13.3	14.9	14.0	15.7
1951	16.1	15.0	18.2	16.5
1952	15.5	14.6	17.3	16.9
1953	13.0	15.0	15.1	16.4
1954	16.5	14.6	16.7	15.1
1955	14.3	14.7	13.4	14.3
1956	13.2	13.5	12.8	14.2
1957	13.0	13.4	16.3	12.9
1958	13.9	14.3	12.4	12.9
1959	16.1	15.0	12.7	—

Source: Data are from FGV. The deflators used for this table are explained in n. 21 of Chapter V.

TABLE V-8. Share of Corporate Depreciation Allowances and Retained Profits in GNP, 1947–1960

Year	Percent	3-year moving average
1947	6.3	—
1948	6.2	6.3
1949	6.4	6.3
1950	6.4	6.6
1951	7.0	7.0
1952	7.8	7.7
1953	8.3	8.4
1954	9.0	8.7
1955	8.7	8.7
1956	8.4	8.4
1957	8.0	8.5
1958	9.2	8.7
1959	8.8	9.2
1960	9.4	—

Source: Computed from data in *Revista Brasileira de Economia*, 16 (March 1962).

TABLE V-9. Public-Sector Expenditure as a Percentage
of GNP, 1947–1960

Year	Percent	3-year moving average
1947	14.7	—
1948	15.3	15.7
1949	17.2	16.5
1950	17.0	17.5
1951	18.3	17.6
1952	17.6	18.6
1953	19.5	19.1
1954	20.2	19.6
1955	19.0	20.5
1956	22.3	21.7
1957	23.9	23.6
1958	24.7	25.2
1959	27.0	26.5
1960	27.7	—

Sources: Computed from material kindly made available
by Dr. Margaret Hanson Costa of the Center for Fiscal
Studies, FGV. The table includes data for the federal,
state, and local governments, as well as the Social
Security Institutes, the Federal Road-Building Corporation, and the National Development Bank. Government
expenditures for the construction of Brasília were computed from "Gastos Públicos em Brasília," *Conjuntura
Econômica*, 16 (December 1962).

TABLE V-10. Expenditure on Fixed-Capital Formation as a Percentage of Public-Sector Expenditure, 1947–1960

Year	Percent	3-year moving average
1947	15.2	—
1948	19.6	18.9
1949	21.8	21.9
1950	24.5	21.8
1951	19.1	20.8
1952	18.8	18.7
1953	18.3	18.4
1954	18.2	17.8
1955	16.9	16.8
1956	15.4	17.4
1957	22.0	20.2
1958	23.2	22.2
1959	21.3	22.7
1960	23.6	—

Sources: Calculated from data supplied by FGV; "Gastos Públicos em Brasília," *Conjuntura Econômica*, 16 (December 1962); *Revista Brasileira de Economia*, 16 (March 1962).

TABLE V-11. The Relative Price of Construction, 1947–1960 (Index: 1947–1949 = 100)

Year	Relative Price
1947	100
1948	100
1949	100
1950	94
1951	89
1952	87
1953	82
1954	79
1955	80
1956	81
1957	83
1958	85
1959	81
1960	82

Source: Computed from the Wholesale Price Index and from an index of construction costs in Rio de Janeiro, published in *Conjuntura Econômica.*

TABLE V-12. Residential and Nonresidential Construction, 1944–1960 (Index: 1947–1949 = 100)

Year	Residential Construction	Nonresidential Construction
1944	104	63
1945	153	72
1946	179	109
1947	91	140
1948	100	100
1949	109	60
1950	123	59
1951	160	109
1952	177	140
1953	189	147
1954	130	149
1955	93	145
1956	162	134
1957	181	233
1958	123	172
1959	108	145
1960	132	172

Source: Indices 11 and 12 of *Conjuntura Econômica*.

VI

DIVISION OF THE MARKET BETWEEN DOMESTIC
PRODUCTION AND IMPORTS

Let us now consider how the Brazilian market for capital goods was divided between domestic producers and importation. We will first discuss the degree of import substitution that in fact occurred, and then the factors—price, quality, international specialization, and suppliers' credits—that have affected competition with imports.

THE DOMESTIC INDUSTRY'S SHARE OF THE MARKET

Data on the share of domestic output in all purchases of producers' equipment during this period are presented in Table VI–1.

TABLE VI-1. Domestic Industry's Share of the Brazilian Market for Producers' Equipment, 1947–1959

Year	Percent	3-year moving average
1947	56	—
1948	61	61
1949	65	65
1950	71	67
1951	65	67
1952	65	68
1953	75	68
1954	71	74
1955	77	76
1956	79	75
1957	70	74
1958	72	72
1959	75	—

Source: Computed from FGV data on the annual value of producers' equipment supplied from domestic sources and from importation.

As we see, even in the late 1940's, the domestic industry supplied over 60 percent of the market for equipment in Brazil.[1] By 1957–1959, its share had reached approximately 75 percent.[2] This increase in the domestic industry's market share occurred in the midst of a general increase in demand for equipment. In 1959, the last year of the time series, the value of equipment supplied to the Brazilian economy was approximately 115 percent higher than in 1947.[3]

TABLE VI-2. Percent of Expenditure on Equipment Supplied by Imports in Brazil and Argentina, 1947–1959

Period	Brazil	Argentina
1947–1949	39	74
1950–1952	33	60
1953–1955	26	49
1956–1958	26	42
1959	25	32

Sources: For Argentina, Carlos Diaz-Alejandro, "Relative Prices and Capital Formation in the Argentine Republic," mimeographed (Yale University, Economic Growth Center, 1965), Tables 1 and 8. For Brazil, data from FGV. Choice of periods was dictated by the periodization used by Diaz.

As Table VI–2 indicates, the domestic industry supplied a much larger share of the market for equipment, especially at the begin-

1. In addition to its time trend, the series shows some fluctuations, in particular a decline in the domestic industry's market share in 1951–1952 and in 1957–1958. As discussed below, Brazilian demand for imported capital goods has been highly dependent on the availability of foreign credits (commercial and official) and direct foreign private investment. The 1951–1952 rise in equipment imports resulted largely from the availability of commercial credits during the Korean War coffee boom. The rise in equipment imports in 1957–1959 was made possible through increases in foreign capital inflow from all three sources.

2. During this period the domestic industry was open to price competition from imports, so that its prices could not diverge from world market levels. Hence the increase in value terms of the domestic industry's market share was not due to a movement of relative prices in which its prices rose more than import prices.

3. Calculated from FGV data on domestic equipment supply. The deflator used was index 63, "Metallurgical Products," of *Conjuntura Econômica*.

ning of this period, than was the case in Argentina, another country for which statistics are available.[4]

PRICE COMPETITION WITH IMPORTS

Price competition with imports has been affected by three factors: domestic prices, foreign prices, and import terms, that is, the exchange rate and government protectionist measures.

In the years 1945–1962, most equipment imports entered Brazil without tariff or other import restrictions, and indeed under a preferential exchange rate. Even in the middle and late 1950's, when tariff legislation was enacted, its effects were usually negated by other legislative and administrative measures. After 1953, however, a new factor conditioned the domestic industry's competition with imports—a downward trend in the real dollar/cruzeiro exchange rate for imports. Most equipment imports still came in without restrictions and under the preferential exchange rate; but the downward pressures on the cruzeiro were so severe that this rate, too, depreciated much more rapidly than internal costs rose. As a result, relative prices moved further in favor of local producers, and stimulated domestic manufacture of many new products that had previously been imported.

Although the domestic industry was able to compete with imports in price, and as we will see in quality too, the extent of import substitution has remained much smaller than for all other Brazilian industries. Even in 1963–1964, when tariffs on equipment imports were for the first time applied extensively, a sizable volume of imports continued. These were in products which, because of their pattern of specialization, Brazilian firms did not produce, and especially because of the availability of foreign suppliers' credits on terms which appeared more favorable than those offered in Brazil.

4. In the heavy-engineering products sector, the percentage of the market supplied by domestic producers was, for reasons we will consider below, smaller, approximately 55% in 1964. This was computed from the import data available in *Comércio Exterior, 1964* (Rio de Janeiro; IBGE, 1966) and from a figure on domestic production, published in ECLA, "Brasil: La Exportación de Manufacturas, sus Antecedentes y sus Possibilidades," mimeographed (Santiago, Chile, 1966), p. 26.

1945–1953

During the period 1945–1953, equipment imports were permitted to enter the country without restrictions.[5] Indeed, throughout these years such imports were subsidized. The 1945 exchange rate (which was already overvalued[6]) was maintained unchanged at a time when the internal price level almost doubled and when national income and demand for imports were rising rapidly.[7]

This exchange-rate policy was dictated by the belief that total foreign exchange receipts and imports were maximized by an overvalued rate, because of price inelasticity of demand for the country's principal export, coffee.[8] To deal with the excess demand for imports that ensued because of over-valuation, the government attempted to promote domestic production of many articles previously imported. In this process, foreign exchange was made available without restriction for equipment imports, which were accorded highest priority in order to facilitate domestic production of other items, largely consumer goods, that were being struck off the import list. Subsidization of equipment imports through preferential treatment has been a traditional Brazilian policy tool for promoting economic development, and it was applied liberally throughout these years.[9]

Despite the absence of restrictions on imports and the over-valued exchange rate, the domestic capital goods industry was, as Table VI–3 indicates, sufficiently competitive to expand output very

5. The only restrictions on capital goods imports during this period were some relatively minor ones, under the "Law of Similars." These applied to only a few products and were often suspended in administrative practice.

6. The exchange rate had been pegged at the 1939 level even though internal prices had risen almost twice as much as in the United States, Brazil's principal foreign supplier.

7. Between 1945 and 1953, Brazilian national income increased 71% (calculated from data in Grupo Misto BNDE-CEPAL, *Análise e Projeções do Desenvolvimento Econômico* [Rio de Janeiro, 1957], p. 81, Table III). In the same period, the purchasing-power parity rate vis-à-vis the United States rose 50%. (This figure is from Octavio Dias Carneiro, "Past Trends of Structural Relationships in the Economic Evolution of Brazil, 1920–1965," mimeographed [Cambridge, Mass.: Center for International Affairs, Harvard University, 1966], Table XXVI.)

8. The price elasticity of demand for coffee has been estimated at 0.25 in *F.A.O. Monthly Bulletin* (October 1954). Moreover, a devaluation of the cruzeiro that lowered the dollar price of coffee to foreign importers would undoubtedly be followed by retaliation and competitive devaluation by other suppliers. Under such conditions, it was believed that exchange-rate depreciation would not greatly increase the supply of foreign exchange and imports. Brazilian exchange-rate policy is discussed in greater detail in chapters 2 and 5 of Nathaniel H. Leff, *Economic Policy-Making and Development in Brazil* (New York, 1968).

9. See the historical material presented in Nícia Vilela Luz, *A Luta pela Industrialização do Brasil* (São Paulo, 1963).

TABLE VI-3. Growth of Output of the Brazilian Capital Goods Industry, 1945–1954

Year	Quantum of domestic capital goods output (Index: 1945 = 100)	Annual change in output (Percent)
1945	100	—
1946	145	45
1947	202	39
1948	172	− 15
1949	208	22
1950	232	44
1951	311	34
1952	358	16
1953	374	4
1954	427	15

Source: Calculated from Grupo Misto BNDE-CEPAL, *Análise e Projeções do Desenvolvimento Econômico* (Rio de Janeiro, 1957), p. 88, Table XIII.

rapidly. Moreover, this growth was achieved from a significant base level, for as early as 1949 value added in the domestic capital goods industries amounted to approximately 306 million dollars.[10] Not only was the industry able to grow rapidly in absolute terms, but, as indicated earlier, it also increased its share of the market.

To achieve this growth in the face of unrestricted price competition with imports, the domestic industry must have been operating under competitive cost conditions.[11] Furthermore, there are no a priori reasons for assuming that the Brazilian industry should not

10. This is calculated from the 1949 figures in the *Censo Industrial*. The exchange rate used for the conversion to dollars is the average import rate, i.e., the amount of cruzeiros paid by importers to the Monetary Authority, divided by the dollar value of imports.

11. The same picture of zero or negative rates of protection is borne out if we consider effective protection, i.e., take into account the duties on the industry's raw materials. As noted below, steel plate and bars, the industry's main raw materials, have been supplied at approximately world market price levels. Nonferrous metals and special alloys, however, have had high (50–100%) tariffs, and have been supplied internally at prices above world market levels. (See EPEA, *Siderugia, Metais Não-Ferrosos: Diagnóstico Preliminar* [Rio de Janeiro: Ministério de Planejamento, 1966], pp. 97–124; and ECLA, *Basic Equipment in Brazil* [*The Manufacture of Industrial Machinery and Equipment in Latin America*, vol. 1 (New York: United Nations, 1963)], p. 60.) Capital goods manufacturers were able to import their own equipment at the preferential exchange-rate. This subsidy, however, affected only a fraction of their total costs, while it lowered the full price of their overseas competitors' products.

have been competitive with world prices for many equipment products. Steel plate and bars, the industry's principal raw material, have been supplied from the Volta Redonda Steel Mill at prices competitive with world market levels.[12] Production of mechanical equipment, even of series-made products, is also relatively labor-intensive, both in Brazil and in the advanced countries, so that Brazilian firms had the advantage of lower wage costs.[13] In addition, the size of the Brazilian equipment market was probably large enough for producers to benefit from many economies external to the firm or to the industry, for by 1949 gross sales of the domestic industry were approximately 750 million dollars.[14]

Finally, the disadvantage of the over-valued and fixed exchange rate was to a certain extent mitigated by the price inflation in the machinery industry of the United States, Brazil's principal foreign supplier. Between 1945 and 1952, prices in the American industry rose 69 percent, helping the Brazilian producers maintain their market position despite internal inflation.[15] Although no index of Brazilian equipment prices exists, we can gain some idea of their evolution from the behavior of the price index for metallurgical products. These are the main raw materials for equipment production, and since the equipment industry's workers belong to the same trade union as those of the metals industry, their wages also move together.[16] Table VI–4 compares the rise of Brazilian metals prices and American machinery prices in the period 1945–1953. This rise in United States machinery prices helped the Brazilian

12. Information is from foreign steel importers in Brazil. Cf. ECLA, *Basic Equipment in Brazil*, p. 60. Brazilian tariff legislation does impose high duties on steel, but these have been used to counter foreign dumping, and have generally not affected internal steel prices. See EPEA, *Siderugia, Metais Não-Ferrosos*, p. 66.

13. See Economic Commission for Europe, "International Trade in Products of the Mechanical and Electrical Engineering Industries," mimeographed (Paris, 1963), p. 33. In Brazil, the ratio of labor costs to value added was approximately 40% higher for the mechanical industry than for the all-industry average. This was computed from data in the 1950 portion of the *Censo Industrial*. For similar data in other years during the 1950's see Werner Baer, *Industrialization and Economic Development in Brazil* (Homewood, Ill., 1965), p. 120, Table 5–11.

14. Computed from FGV data on domestic equipment production. The exchange rate used for the conversion was the average import rate.

15. This is calculated from data in the U.S. Bureau of Labor Statistics *Bulletin*, No. 1214, p. 32.

16. Wages in the metallurgical and equipment industries have been led by the wage policy of the National Steel Company, a public-sector corporation, which in turn has passed on wage increases in its product prices, for which it is also the market leader.

TABLE VI-4. U.S. Machinery Prices and Brazilian Metallurgical Prices, 1945–1953 (Index: 1945 = 100)

Year	(a) Brazilian metallurgical prices	(b) U.S. machinery prices	(c) Relative prices (a/b)
1945	100	100	100
1946	111	111	100
1947	121	129	94
1948	126	140	90
1949	142	147	96
1950	150	151	100
1951	176	165	107
1952	179	169	106
1953	263	171	154

Sources: The Brazilian metallurgical-products price index used is index 63 of *Conjuntura Econômica*. The American machinery prices index is from the U.S. Bureau of Labor Statistics *Bulletin*, No. 1214.

domestic industry maintain its competitive position until the 1953 devaluation.

DEVELOPMENTS IN THE 1954–1962 PERIOD

In October 1953, Instruction 70 of the Monetary Authority established an across-the-board devaluation and a multiple exchange-rate system. In an effort to promote capital formation, equipment imports were still accorded preferential treatment, and imports were made at a special exchange rate, the *custo de câmbio*. Although this rate was "preferential," the other products, notably petroleum, included in the category took so large a portion of all imports that the favored rate was not too far from the average import exchange rate—that is, the cruzeiro cost of all imports divided by their dollar cost. And although the government tried to maintain a special rate for high-priority imports, this rate too followed the cruzeiro's rapid depreciation. Table VI–5 presents annual data on the value of the preferential rate as a percentage of the average import rate. In the period as a whole, the preferential rate averaged 78 percent of the annual average rate.

Another development affecting price competition with imports was the institution, in 1956, of tariffs averaging 45 percent ad

TABLE VI-5. Brazilian Preferential Exchange Rate as a Percentage of Average Import Exchange Rate, 1954–1960

Year	Percent
1954	76
1955	65
1956	75
1957	82
1958	91
1959	83
1960	73

Source: Data on preferential and average import exchange rates were supplied by the Research Division, SUMOC.

valorem on many equipment products.[17] Import prohibitions were also applied to some equipment products for which domestic supply capacity existed. In principle, these protectionist measures insulated the domestic industry from price competition with imports. In practice, however, their effect was largely nullified by other legislation, and by a great deal of administrative flexibility in their application, so that competitive pressures on domestic producers continued.[18]

Most of the major purchasers of equipment were, by other policy decisions, exempted from tariffs and import restrictions, as the government attempted to promote investment and development in key industries. The legislation which established government economic corporations in such areas as petroleum, steel, railways, and electricity gave them the right of duty-free importation. Because, as noted in Chapter V, the public sector accounted for more than 40 percent of gross fixed-capital formation during these years, the exemptions amounted to a large share of the total equipment market. Furthermore, in the private sector, companies

17. Data on tariffs was supplied by the Research Division of SUMOC. Cf. also Santiago Macario, "Proteccionismo y Industrialización en América Latina," *Boletín Económico de América Latina*, 9 (March 1964), 72, Table 3.

18. Material in this and subsequent paragraphs is based on interviews with former members of the National Tariff Council.

in such important equipment-using industries as electricity, metallurgy, chemicals, cement, paper, and automobiles were usually given exemption from tariffs. The development credentials of these industries were considered as good as, if not better than, those of the capital goods industry, so that liberal treatment was accorded to their imports. Foreign private investors were also allowed tariff exemption. The military, too, enjoyed duty-free import privileges; and in response to special political pressures, the president on occasion intervened to extend still further the list of exemptions. For example, in the late 1950's and early 1960's, as Brazil sought a more "independent" foreign policy and trade delegations from the Eastern European countries visited the country, import restrictions were often waived for their equipment sales.

The effects of tariffs and import restrictions were further limited by the policy adopted with regard to foreign suppliers' credits. Believing that such financing made a net addition to the country's capital formation, the government suspended import restrictions for equipment supplied with foreign credits. By administrative decision, other equipment imports were also exempted from tariffs if the purchaser could convince the National Tariff Council that the cost of import duties would prevent him from carrying out his investment project.[19]

Although tariffs and import restrictions were generally not applied, the competitive position of the Brazilian industry was strengthened by the depreciation, in real terms, of the exchange rate for imports. Because of the severe pressures on the Brazilian balance of payments, the external depreciation of the cruzeiro proceeded more rapidly than internal inflation. Since most equipment imports had duty-free status and preferential exchange-rate treatment, they constitute the most relevant import category

19. This paradox of applying protection to the equipment industries in principle, but suspending it by other measures and even according these imports preferential exchange-rate treatment, reflects Brazilian policymakers' fundamental ambivalence concerning the value of a domestic capital goods industry. On the one hand, they wanted to promote domestic equipment production. On the other hand, cheapening the cost of equipment importation had always been a policy instrument for promoting development. Restricting equipment imports, particularly if supplied with foreign credits, was expected to have a detrimental effect on capital formation and growth. To my knowledge, no systematic study was undertaken to examine the assumptions behind these decisions and provide the basis for a more consistent policy.

TABLE VI-6. Preferential-Rate Machinery-Import Prices and Domestic Metal-lurgical Prices, 1953–1961

Year	(a) Brazilian metallurgical prices (Index)	(b) Cost of imported equipment (at preferential exchange rate and duty-free) (Index)	(c) Relative prices (a/b)
1953	100	100	100
1954	125	138	91
1955	144	157	91
1956	183	249	74
1957	193	292	66
1958	278	415	67
1959	399	629	64
1960	423	629	68
1961	548	943	58

Source: Column (a) is index 63 of *Conjuntura Econômica*. To obtain column (b) the index of United States machinery prices was multiplied by an index of the *câmbio de custo*, the preferential exchange rate, for which annual data were kindly provided by the Research Division of SUMOC.

for a comparison with domestic prices. Table VI–6 compares the evolution of prices for such machinery imports with the price index for Brazilian metallurgical products, thus giving an idea of the movement of relative prices.

Even without tariff duties and with the subsidized exchange rate, the cost of imported equipment rose much more rapidly than domestic metallurgical prices. Because of the increased real cost of imports, relative prices came to favor domestic production for many products that were previously not produced in Brazil and with which, given an unaltered real exchange rate, imports might have been competitive.[20]

Finally, the chronic foreign-exchange shortage has also favored local producers in other ways. Equipment purchasers often turned to domestic producers in reaction to the increasing costs of delays, unpredictability, and bureaucratic frustration involved in queuing

20. Substantial inflation in American machinery prices also continued during the latter half of the 1950's. See Thomas Wilson, "An Analysis of the Inflation in Machinery Prices," Joint Economic Committee, U.S. Congress (Washington, D.C.: Government Printing Office, 1959).

for administrative allocations of foreign-exchange and import licenses.[21] The relative ease of domestic spare-parts supply also contrasted with possible bottleneck effects involved in reliance on importation or with the high costs of maintaining adequate replacement inventories. Interviews with equipment purchasers indicate that they consider these costs as important as the higher relative purchase price of imported equipment in determining their shift to domestic suppliers.

QUALITY COMPETITION WITH IMPORTS

The quality of domestic production has also affected the division of the market with foreign suppliers. In the industry's early days, it often competed with imports largely as a low-quality producer, offering goods which appealed to some segments of the market because their price was also lower than imported products. In the postwar period, however, local firms have improved their technical standards, narrowing or erasing the quality differential between local and world market quality levels.[22]

In the heavy-engineering products sector, firms have been able to meet the international standards required for boiler products by *Lloyd's Register of Shipping*. The same is true for mechanical products with respect to standards set by the international engineering firms that have taken responsibility for many local engineering projects. In the capital goods industry as a whole, quality standards have improved as foreign firms established Brazilian manufacturing subsidiaries, taking due care to maintain their international quality reputation. (Indeed, as noted in Chapter II, foreign firms have sometimes been so careful not to lower quality standards and jeopardize their international reputation that they have weakened their position within the Brazilian market.) Some companies under local ownership and management also achieved standards enabling them to compete effectively with these foreign firms.

This improvement in the capital goods industry's technical standards seems to have been a consequence of the growth in the

21. This material is from interviews with major equipment importers in São Paulo.
22. Some domestic capital goods producers have participated in the world market, exporting their products to the advanced countries. More extensive exportation has not occurred largely because of exchange-rate over-valuation and imperfections in the international equipment market, as discussed in Chap. V, n. 13.

market for quality products to a size sufficient to justify investment in domestic capacity for higher-quality production and control. With growing national income and aggregate demand for equipment, and with (as noted) a shift in demand toward better technical standards, the market for better-quality products increased. At the same time, the chronic balance-of-payments problem, and the movement of relative prices in favor of domestic producers that it entailed, meant that on the basis of price considerations, this large and growing market could be supplied from local rather than overseas sources. Growth in individual product markets also enabled local firms to overcome indivisibilities in personnel and equipment necessary for higher-quality production and testing. Finally, as we will see in the next chapter, domestic competition also put strong pressures on firms to achieve higher-quality production.[23]

Technical standards have also improved because of developments external to the industry and its market. By universal testimony, the establishment of the Brazilian automotive industry in the late 1950's had as one of its side-effects a marked improvement in the quality of production in the capital goods industry.[24] The automotive companies, most of whom were foreign, attempted to maintain technical standards similar to those of the advanced countries, and thus they created a new market for quality forgings, castings, and other components. In response to this demand, many foreign companies with the equipment, personnel, and know-how necessary for higher-quality production also established Brazilian manufacturing plants. When these plants were installed, however, their capacity usually turned out to be greater than demands of the automotive industry, and they turned to supply quality components to the capital goods industry as well. The automotive companies were also instrumental in raising the technical standards of suppliers under domestic ownership. Because of their strong market position as large clients for standardized components, they could exert sufficient pressures on their suppliers to ensure com-

23. Claude Machline, in a study of quality control practices in São Paulo industry, "O Contrôle de Qualidade na Indústria Paulista," *Revista de Administração de Empresas*, 1 (January-April 1962), 47–49, also stresses competition among sellers as a major determinant of company measures to raise quality standards.
24. The source for what follows here is interview material obtained from several of the automotive companies, and from metallurgical companies supplying both the automotive and the capital goods industry.

pliance with standards. As a result, they overcame indivisibilities that had previously inhibited firms from investing in capacity— both in personnel and in equipment—for quality production and control facilities. The automotive companies also made available laboratories and technical personnel that enabled some of their smaller suppliers to attain better standards.

In addition to these changes which led to the development of higher technical standards within the capital goods industry and among its suppliers, clients' subjective attitudes toward the quality of domestic equipment products have also changed. Market acceptance of the industry's products had always been inhibited because of clients' hesitations concerning the quality of locally made products. This was "the mentality," often cited by domestic firms, that deemed imports invariably superior to local products.[25] This attitude was often justified in the earlier period. But it some- times lagged behind the improvement of objective standards, because clients were unwilling to incur the risks of switching to new suppliers, or to pay the information costs of eliminating uncertainties by testing the quality of local products. In the post- war period, this bias against local products was generally overcome. The movement of relative prices in favor of domestic industry has usually been substantial enough to overcome prejudices or justify investigation of local products. In some cases, capital goods producers have themselves had their product tested at an indepen- dent laboratory such as the São Paulo Institute of Technological Research.

DIVISION OF THE MARKET WITH IMPORTS, 1962–1964

The domestic industry's ability to compete with imports in price and quality has led to its relatively large share of the market that we noted in Table VI–1. At the same time, however, imports have continued to take more than a negligible share of the market. In 1962–1964, annual imports amounted to some 340 million dollars, or approximately 20 percent of the supply of all producers' equip-

---

25. This "mentality" often existed in connection with consumer products, too, and local firms which have attained high-quality standards have sometimes disguised their goods as imports, to achieve market acceptance and sell at the higher price usually available for imports.

ment.[26] The share of imports in Brazilian equipment supply is higher and has declined much less in the postwar period that the import coefficients for all other Brazilian industries. Table VI–7 highlights this situation by comparing the import coefficient of the mechanical industry, a sub-category within producers' equipment, with that of other Brazilian industries.

TABLE VI-7. Imports as a Percentage of All Domestic Consumption, Selected Industries

Industry	1949	1958	1961
Metallurgical	22	12	12
Electrical material	45	13	17
Transport equipment	57	31	19
Chemical and pharmaceutical	29	20	17
Paper	10	4	4
Rubber products	10	5	7
Textiles	6	1	1
Mechanical products	64	42	46

Source: "Auge y Declinación del Proceso de Sustitución de Importaciones en el Brasil," *Boletín Económico de América Latina,* 9 (March 1964), Table 25.

This continuing high level of imports is the result of two factors. First, for imports available with foreign suppliers' credits on apparently very favorable terms, domestic demand has been inelastic with respect to relative product prices. Second, because of the domestic industry's pattern of specialization, it is not equally competitive with imports for all products. Despite increasing diversification of supply, the local industry is far from producing the full range of goods demanded. Although with economic development and enlargement in the size of the market many new products have come to be produced domestically, demand has grown for other products which have been supplied by importation.

Imports have continued, for example, for highly specialized products, where the domestic market is still too small to attract local producers. Furthermore, because of their comparative advantage, local manufacturers have preferred to concentrate on

26. Data are from the Research Division of SUMOC and from IBRD, "Manufacturing Industry" ("Current Economic Position and Prospects of Brazil," vol. 5, mimeographed [Washington, D.C., February 1965]) Annexes A, C.

lighter products, leaving the heavier and/or more specialized products to be supplied by importation.[27] Despite trends such as we noted in engineering products (that is, toward production of heavier goods), Brazilian equipment producers still manufacture a lighter product line than firms in the advanced countries. For example, a 1961 survey of Brazilian machine-tool companies showed that the average weight of the machines produced was less than 1 ton, as compared with 2.5 tons for imported machine tools.[28] Firms making other products testify to a similar specialization on lighter products.

This division of labor has occurred because, on the supply side, heavier products are often more capital-intensive in their production. Moreover, the market for the lighter and less specialized products has usually been larger, and local producers have preferred to concentrate on the products with the largest domestic demand.[29] Domestic producers have also been encouraged in this policy by the government, which, in legislating tariff protection, has preferred products with the largest domestic market.[30] As a result, import substitution has taken place largely in lighter and less specialized equipment, while imports have come more and more to consist of specialized and heavier products. Table VI–8, which presents some data on this trend, shows that in the course of this period the percentage of "heavy" equipment increased considerably.[31] Actually, the data of Table VI–8 understate this trend, for within other categories—for example, "electrical equipment"—the share of the heavier and more specialized equipment also rose notably.[32]

Finally, a large volume of imports has continued for equipment supplied with foreign credits. In this case, too, demand has been

27. The material that follows is based on interviews with companies in the heavy-engineering sector, in machine-tool manufacturing, and in diesel-engine production.

28. *Las Máquinas-Herramientas en el Brasil* (*La Fabricación de Maquinarias y Equipos Industriales en América Latina*, vol. 2 [New York: United Nations, 1962]), p. 41.

29. ECLA, *Basic Equipment in Brazil*, p. 38.

30. According to ECLA, *Basic Equipment in Brazil*, p. 67, Brazilian ad valorem duty rates are about twice as high on lighter machinery imports as on heavier items in the same product line.

31. "Heavy Mechanical Equipment" in the ECLA source is used in contradistinction to "Medium and Light Equipment." Although the basis for categorization is not explained, the general implication is clear and accords with abundant testimony from domestic producers and their clients.

32. "Auge y Declinación del Proceso de Sustitución de Importaciones en el Brasil," *Boletín Económico de América Latina*, 9 (March 1964), 36.

TABLE VI-8. Percentage of "Heavy" Mechanical Equipment in All Equipment Imports to Brazil, 1948–1961

Year	Percent	Year	Percent
1948	15	1955	29
1949	23	1956	22
1950	21	1957	28
1951	21	1958	26
1952	23	1959	20
1953	32	1960	34
1954	34	1961	32

Source: Calculated from data in "Auge y Declinación del Proceso de Sustitución de Importaciones en el Brasil," *Boletín Económico de América Latina*, 9 (March 1964), pp. 34–38, Tables 19, 20, 23.

unresponsive to the price differential between domestic and imported equipment. Foreign equipment loans have usually been at interest rates of 9–10 percent, over periods of up to five years. In both respects, the terms have appeared far more advantageous than anything available from domestic lenders.[33] Domestic investors have therefore preferred to borrow abroad for financing of their equipment purchases. Because these credits have been tied to purchase of foreign products, however, Brazilian investors have also purchased imported equipment.[34] They were encouraged in this policy by the government, which saw in such suppliers' loans a cheap source of financing for domestic capital formation, and which made available foreign exchange for servicing these debts at the preferential exchange rate.

Table VI–9 shows the relative importance of foreign-financed equipment imports in all equipment imports by domestic investors—that is, total equipment imports minus equipment imported by direct foreign investors. As we see, foreign-financed equipment accounted for an extremely large share of all equipment imports by Brazilian investors: for the nine-year period as a whole,

33. See, however, the discussion of foreign and domestic credit costs, pp. 152–154 below.

34. During this period, most of this financing was furnished by governmental institutions such as the American EXIMBANK, where loans were tied to equipment of national origin as a matter of policy, perhaps because the market imperfection introduced by tied credits permits higher returns to national producing firms.

TABLE VI-9. Foreign-Financed Equipment Imports as
a Percentage of all Equipment Imported by Domestic
Investors, 1955–1963

Year	Percent	Year	Percent
1955	38	1960	71
1956	62	1961	70
1957	89	1962	69
1958	97	1963	59
1959	89		

Source: Calculated from data kindly supplied by the Research Division of SUMOC.

it amounted to 71 percent of all imported equipment purchased by
domestic investors. In heavy-engineering products, the incidence
of imports with foreign financing has been even greater, explaining
in part the sector's above-average import coefficient. In
determining the allocation of foreign credits, the government
accorded a very high priority to the metallurgical, electricity, and
chemical industries which are the sector's clients.[35]

Because of the availability of foreign finance tied to equipment
imports, the extent of import substitution has been significantly
lower in equipment than in all other Brazilian industries. As noted
in Table VI–7, the import coefficient for the mechanical industry
has been much higher than in industries such as metallurgy,
chemicals, and paper.[36] Those industries may present greater
production problems, such as more capital-intensive technology or
larger optimal scale, but they do not have to compete with imports
which are preferred by clients because they bring with them their
own financing.[37]

Because of these credits, imports have continued for equipment
products which domestic firms do produce and in which they could
compete under favorable relative-price and quality conditions.

35. See the data on government allocation of foreign suppliers' credits in "Fifteen Years of
Economic Policy in Brazil," *Economic Bulletin for Latin America*, 9 (November 1964), 174–175.

36. Of course, one reason why the import coefficient has been relatively low in those
industries is precisely because it has been so high for producers' equipment. Equipment
imports supported by foreign investment credits—which were particularly high in those
industries—contributed significantly to increasing domestic supply capacity and thus lowered
their import coefficients.

37. As mentioned earlier, government policy has reserved foreign supplier credits almost
exclusively for equipment imports.

Indeed, in some industries imports have been maintained even for products in which local producers have had a high degree of excess capacity. As the São Paulo State Bank described the situation of the mechanical industry in 1960: "A considerable part of installed capacity is not used, remaining idle. There are several reasons for the industry's excess capacity. Among them we should note the lack of adequate finance for sales and the ease of obtaining foreign exchange favors and tariff reductions, which contribute toward accentuating the preference for imported products."[38]

Because of tied financing, equipment imports continued at a relatively high level in 1962–1964, despite several developments which might have been expected to raise the domestic market share. First, direct foreign investment, which had previously constituted another form of capital inflow tied to equipment imports, shrank sharply in response to unsettled political conditions. Secondly, after 1962, in an effort to deal with the drastic balance-of-payments situation by promoting further import substitution in capital goods, the National Tariff Council began increasingly to apply the country's high tariffs on equipment. Finally, as the inflation reached annual rates greater than 50 percent, the monetary authorities instituted a system of import deposits. Since the value of these deposits depreciated rapidly, they, too, constituted a heavy charge on importation, increasing the price advantage of domestic producers.

Despite these changes affecting price competition with imports, the domestic industry did not greatly expand its share of the market.[39] This experience suggests that in the present range, the elasticity of substitution with respect to relative prices between domestic and foreign supply is too low to generate further import substitution unless the industry can compete with imports in terms of suppliers' credits. Other studies of the Brazilian capital goods industry have also come to this conclusion.[40] Let us therefore consider the situation affecting Brazilian domestic long-term (five-year) credits in some detail.

38. *Relatório da Directoria, Banco do Estado de São Paulo, S.A.* (São Paulo, 1961), p. 32 (my translation). For information about a similar situation in shipbuilding, see "A Fabrição no Brasil dos Equipamentos para as Indústrias de Base: Discussão," *Boletim da Associação Brasileira de Metais,* 19 (January 1963), 91.

39. See IBRD, "Current Economic Situation," chap. V, Annex C.

40. Cf. ECLA, *Basic Equipment in Brazil,* pp. 6–7, 69–71; *Las Máquinas-Herramientas en el Brasil,* p. 46.

PROSPECTS FOR FURTHER EXPANSION OF THE DOMESTIC INDUSTRY'S MARKET SHARE

LONG-TERM EQUIPMENT FINANCE IN BRAZIL

Although finance of domestic capital goods purchases might appear a logical task for a development bank, the Brazilian National Development Bank did very little in this direction, and it reaffirmed this negative policy decision as late as 1963.[41] The Bank preferred to concentrate its limited resources on a few high-priority sectors, notably electricity and steel, which it has considered crucial for the development of the economy as a whole.[42] Indeed, the Bank itself relied heavily on foreign-financed equipment imports for its projects in these areas.[43] The Development Bank has also feared that financing of domestic equipment purchases in other industries would merely substitute for—rather than add to—savings resources which such investors would otherwise mobilize on their own.[44]

Brazilian commercial banks have also not taken a prominent role in financing of medium- and long-term equipment purchases. This has usually been discussed in terms of institutional rigidities

41. Banco Nacional do Desenvolvimento Econômico, *XII Exposição sôbre o Programa de Reaparelhamento Econômico* (Rio de Janeiro, 1964), p. 39.
42. The material in this paragraph is based on interviews with officials of the Bank.
43. The Bank's administrators seem to have adopted the following implicit model in choosing this policy. Suppose that all investment projects—e.g., in steel and electricity—have two components: equipment, for which foreign finance is available, and construction, for which domestic resources must be used. If we represent different levels of capital formation by the different isoquants, we can say that the Development Bank wanted to reach the highest isoquant compatible with its own resources available for construction. This would lead to attaining the highest possible level of capital formation rather than achieving a lower level of investment, but with greater participation of the domestic equipment industry.

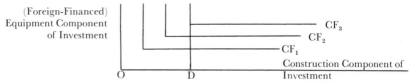

OD = Development Bank's own resources

44. The assumption behind this policy has been that investment needs of many domestic industries in the private sector—e.g., textiles and food processing—are limited. Growth of the domestic industry's share of the market through import substitution has already taken place. Consequently, it is believed that demand will grow only relatively slowly in accordance with aggregate income growth and the income elasticity of demand. Hence, profit reinvestment is considered to provide sufficient resources for their expansion, and provision of capital from other sources—e.g., the Development Bank—would supposedly only reduce their internal savings.

("the failure of the banking system to adapt from the needs of a colonial exporting country to a modern industrial economy") and of factors on the supply side that have deterred Brazilian banks from offering loans either for time periods or at interest rates comparable with those available abroad.[45] As the conventional argument runs: in an inflationary environment, banks cannot attract medium- and long-term deposits either from personal savings or from corporate reserves, since no one wants to remain liquid during inflation. Hence the banks lack the time deposits to serve as the basis for such loans. They are, moreover, regulated by a legal provision which prohibits nominal interest charges higher than 12 percent, a rate well below recent rates of inflation. Although the banks circumvent this provision through "service" charges, this has reinforced their preference for short-term loans, with their higher turnover and income from transactions payments.

These arguments are not entirely convincing. First, the banking system has been willing and able to play a prominent role in financing another long-term investment, real-estate construction. In addition to their relatively long finance period, such investments have in common with heavy equipment a high unit cost and a long production period, features which have been claimed to add to the difficulties of finding adequate financing for the equipment industries.[46]

Secondly, as is sometimes recognized, other financial inter-mediaries, the "financial corporations," have emerged parallel to the banking system.[47] By paying high nominal and reasonable real rates of interest, these financial intermediaries have been able to attract medium-term deposits and have made medium- and long-

45. E.g., ECIA, *Basic Equipment in Brazil*, pp. 69–71.

46. This refers to another argument often heard among Brazilian capital goods producers and repeated by the ECLA report: "Financing of the production and sales of the basic equipment industry . . . entails long-term credits and low rates of interest owing to the high unit value of the articles concerned or the . . . time-consuming process of their manufacture . . . The prices of heavy equipment would not stand the high interest rates" (*Basic Equipment in Brazil*, p. 70). That is, because of the high unit value of equipment and the financing required during the relatively long gestation period of production (from 6 to 24 months), interest charges to the purchaser for financing over a 3- to 5-year period would be very onerous, making purchase unattractive. As stated, this argument is either fallacious or a plea for subsidization of the industry and/or its clients. First, it is not clear why the real return to users of the equipment should not increase commensurately with its high unit value. Alternatively, the argument implies that returns in client industries do not justify equipment purchases if real market rates of interest must be taken into account in the investment decision.

47. *Basic Equipment in Brazil*, p. 70.

term loans at charges above the legal maximum.[48] Since long-term financing has been available both from the banks and from the parallel financial market to clients who could pay reasonable real interest charges, the conditions affecting financing for equipment purchases appear more complex than the conventional arguments allow for. Further explanation seems needed.

In the first place, the returns from some industrial investments would simply not be high enough to bear the cost of real interest charges.[49] This is in contrast with the situation for many real estate borrowers, whose market prospects have been very favorable as a result of the expanding demand for housing and other construction facilities in a rapidly urbanizing society. Perhaps even more important, many domestic equipment purchasers who could bear such interest charges have preferred not to do so, since they had the alternative of borrowing from foreign suppliers at rates which appeared much lower. Other investors, however—for construction, for instance—have not had the option of the apparently cheaper foreign credits; for by a government decision, foreign commercial credits were reserved almost exclusively for equipment imports.

FOREIGN CREDITS AND DOMESTIC CREDITS

In reality, the "cheap" foreign financing preferred by local borrowers and encouraged by the government turned out to be more expensive than the "extortionist" rates charged by local lenders. Overseas debts were contracted in foreign currency, and the difference between the domestic and foreign interest rates was more than offset by the depreciation of the cruzeiro, in real terms, during the loan period.

In the late 1950's and early 1960's, with rapid economic growth and demand pressing upon income-inelastic supply of foreign exchange, the real cost of foreign exchange in Brazil increased sharply, raising with it the cost of servicing overseas debts.[50] This

48. The ECLA report, p. 70, cites nominal interest charges "well above 20% per annum simply because such bodies have to distribute annual dividends far exceeding 12% if they are to attract available savings." Assuming that interest charges were 40% and time-deposits were paid 30%, this was still relatively low in real terms since the annual rate of inflation at that time (1960–1961) was approximately 30%.

49. Cf. the remark to this effect in the ECLA Report, cited in n. 46 above.

50. For a discussion of the depreciation of the real exchange rate in Brazil, see Nathaniel H. Leff, "Export Stagnation and Autarkic Development in Brazil," *The Quarterly Journal of Economics*, 81 (May 1967), 286–301.

exchange premium increased the cost of foreign interest and amortization payments, both for individual firms servicing their equipment loans and for the economy as a whole, inasmuch as the social cost of foreign exchange also increased notably. Table VI–10 shows the annual rise in the exchange rate for foreign equipment loans, until mid-1961 the preferential *câmbio de custo*. The data apply to a five-year loan contracted in 1957, when large-scale drawing on suppliers' credits for equipment imports began.

TABLE VI-10. Annual Real Increase in Private Cost of Foreign Exchange for Servicing Equipment Loans, 1958–1962

Year	Foreign-exchange premium (percent)
1958	20.3
1959	12.9
1960	− 25.0
1961	11.3
1962	55.0

Source: Data on the annual *câmbio de custo* exchange rate, supplied by the Research Division of SUMOC, were deflated by the implicit GNP deflator. From the ensuing exchange rates in constant cruzeiros, annual percentage changes were computed.

With the exception of 1960, when the government was able to maintain a stable exchange rate in a period of rapid internal inflation, the annual increase in real terms has been substantial. Even the efforts at holding the rate stable in 1960 and 1961 were eventually negated, with the large adjustment of 1962. For the period as a whole, the foreign-exchange premium determined by the cruzeiro's real depreciation was 15 percent.

As indicated in Table VI–11, a similar depreciation occurred with the average import exchange rate. Over the period, the average import rate depreciated approximately 10.4 percent. The social cost of foreign exchange to the Brazilian economy increased even more, however. During these years, higher import restrictions were also applied to many consumer and intermediate goods, and this removed considerable pressure of demand from the exchange

TABLE VI-11. Annual Real Increase in Average Cruzeiro/Dollar Exchange Rate for Imports in Brazil, 1958–1962

Year	Foreign-exchange premium (percent)
1958	9.0
1959	25.3
1960	−6.2
1961	10.6
1962	13.2

Source: Data on the average effective exchange rate, the cruzeiro cost of all imports divided by their CIF dollar value, were supplied by the Research Division of SUMOC. The annual foreign-exchange premium was computed by the same procedures as in Table VI-10.

market. Furthermore, since the average exchange rate has shown a consistent upward trend, the *marginal* cost of foreign exchange to the economy probably rose even more than the average.

POSSIBILITIES FOR FURTHER EXPANSION OF THE DOMESTIC INDUSTRY'S MARKET SHARE

This foreign-exchange premium has usually been overlooked in discussion of the competition with foreign equipment supplied by "cheap" credits.[51] If rapid Brazilian aggregate growth continues in the previous pattern of long-term foreign-exchange appreciation, the existence of this premium may permit some further expansion of the domestic industry's share of the market. With an overseas

51. The only exception I found was a statement by J. G. Haenel, who encountered this problem as one of the executives in charge of equipment purchases for the COSIPA steel mill. In a retrospective view, he concluded that finance costs would have been lower had the company borrowed from local "financial corporations" despite their high nominal rates. See "A Fabrição no Brasil dos Equipamentos: Discussão," p. 85. In the early years of extensive use of foreign suppliers' credits, the Monetary Authority sometimes guaranteed a fixed exchange rate, so the practice was entirely rational during those years from the viewpoint of the individual firms. Such guarantees were not continued, however, so that private borrowers did have to pay the foreign-exchange premium in subsequent years. It is not surprising that individual businessmen did not anticipate the decline in the real exchange rate, for this would have required that they project accurately over five years the rate of internal inflation and the external depreciation of the cruzeiro. The failure of the government, with its macro view to notice the phenomenon is surprising, however.

interest rate of 10 percent and a domestic real rate of 20 percent, the difference is offset by a foreign-exchange premium such as prevailed in the 1950's and early 1960's. Hence, if this premium continues over the long-term,[52] domestic capital goods purchasers might well prefer domestic loans to foreign equipment finance. According to local bankers, the supply of credits would be highly elastic at real interest rates of 15-20 percent; so a large volume of resources might respond to finance equipment purchasers who would take into account the real cost of foreign loans.[53] Given the rising social marginal cost of foreign exchange, these considerations probably apply *a fortiori* to the government, both in its fostering of domestic recourse to foreign credits, and its policy (for example, by the Development Bank) regarding the provision of long-term finance for domestic equipment purchases.

As Table VI–12 indicates, in the years 1960–1963, Brazilian equipment imports financed with foreign suppliers' credits averaged

TABLE VI-12. Annual Equipment Imports Financed by Foreign Suppliers' Credits, 1960–1963

Year	Millions of dollars
1960	224
1961	274
1962	246
1963	186

Source: Data supplied by the Research Division of SUMOC.

52. In 1965–1967, however, the situation was reversed, with the depreciation of the real cruzeiro/dollar exchange rate. This occurred because a slackening of aggregate growth checked the demand for imports and the pressure on the exchange rate, while internal inflation continued at annual rates over 25%.

53. Indeed, the *letras de câmbio*, guaranteed short-term lending which provided the highest (pure) return in the Brazilian money market of 1963, rarely paid more than 5% annually in real terms. They were popular as one of the few financial assets whose value kept pace with the inflation. In the heightened inflation of 1964, even these short-term investments paid returns below the annual rate of inflation. See EPEA, *O Mercado Brasileiro de Capitais* (Rio de Janeiro: Ministerio de Planejamento, 1965), pp. 66–67, 70.

approximately 230 million dollars annually.[54] For the Brazilian economy to provide as much equipment finance as has been supplied by foreign lenders, at ceiling output levels and without reducing investment elsewhere in the economy, aggregate savings would have to be raised by approximately 8 percent.[55]

Over the past decade, there have been numerous proposals that the National Development Bank or the São Paulo State Bank finance equipment sales to permit domestic producers to compete with imports in terms of credits. As suggested, if Brazilian long-term development resumes in the pattern of rapidly growing demand pressing on relatively income-inelastic supply of foreign exchange, policy measures might also be justified to correct equipment purchasers' imperfect knowledge concerning future foreign-exchange costs and make them aware that borrowing abroad may involve equal if not higher real rates. It remains to be seen whether any developments in this direction will actually take place and thereby permit some further expansion of the domestic industry's market share.[56] In any case, part of the equipment imported with foreign financing consists of highly specialized products which Brazilian firms do not manufacture. Consequently, even if the market imperfection introduced by credit terms is removed, import substitution will probably still not proceed to the extent characteristic of other Brazilian industries.

54. In 1963 there was a reduction in foreign equipment finance. This was in reaction to the great pressure of short- and medium-term obligations on Brazilian debt-servicing capacity, and to the political conditions which made foreign lenders reluctant to offer additional credits.

55. Equipment purchases have averaged 9% of GNP. Of these, approximately 25% have been imported, of which 70% were obtained with foreign suppliers' credits. Thus foreign suppliers' credits have constituted approximately 1.4% of GNP. Since domestic savings have averaged 17% of GNP, provision of domestic equipment financing in an amount equal to what has come in recently from abroad would entail an 8% increase in domestic savings. Under recent conditions of excess capacity in the capital goods industry, of course, credit creation for this purpose might also go far toward dealing with this problem without a great inflationary impact, for income and savings would rise to justify the increased investment.

56. In late 1964, the Development Bank did establish a small fund, FINAME, to provide some domestic equipment credits.

VII

MARKET STRUCTURE

Having discussed the aggregate demand for equipment in Brazil and the domestic industry's market share, let us now consider the market structure within which firms competed for this demand, in the period 1962–1964. Because of data limitations, our discussion here will be confined to the heavy-engineering products sector, though the picture presented appears valid for other parts of the capital goods industry.[1]

Questions of market structure have sometimes been neglected in discussions of industrial development in less-developed countries. On the one hand, it is often assumed that industrial organization is inevitably monopolistic, either because of a special indisposition of entrepreneurs in underdeveloped countries to competition, or because of structural factors such as economies of scale favoring the first entrant to a market of limited size. Alternatively, it has sometimes been assumed, in Latin America for example, that the monopoly question is somehow less relevant for economic analysis than in the advanced economies where the issue was first posed.

As regards the first point, we will see that firms in this sector do compete actively among themselves. Despite the cartelizing preferences of some of the sector's entrepreneurs, structural conditions such as the free flow of imports, ease of entry, excess capacity, and the market power of clients have forced them to competition. Moreover, concerning the value of a discussion of industrial organization in a less-developed economy, we should point out that once the relevance of a competitive model has been evaluated, subsequent analysis and policy discussions are greatly simplified. Furthermore, any theory of economic development that stresses the importance of externalities must be concerned with the extent

1. As discussed in Chapter I, because available resources did not permit investigation of this subject for the entire capital goods industry, I concentrated on one sector. Scattered interviewing elsewhere in the industry and testimony of other observers suggest that the present discussion also applies to other sectors within the industry. As noted earlier, excess capacity, one of the principal reasons for the sector's active market rivalry, has also developed elsewhere in the industry.

157

to which pecuniary external economies are actually passed on, by competitive pressures, to other sectors of the company.

NATURE OF COMPETITION IN THE SECTOR

The sector's market structure is not, in the strict sense, one of perfect competition. Products are often not homogeneous, and the number of sellers is small enough for individual firms to be aware of the effects of their decisions on other companies and on the whole market. However, this is imperfect competition of an especially aggressive kind, for there is very active rivalry among firms on the basis of prices, quality, and credit.

Price competition appears when firms submit projects for tenders solicited by clients. In these bids, firms calculate their costs and adjust profit margins individually and competitively, for prices are an important consideration in contract awards. Individual firms often feel that they suffer from such price competition and the absence of collusive arrangements, but for reasons examined below, they have not been able to form a stable price-fixing agreement.

Apart from interviews, evidence on the force of price competition comes from several sources. In the period 1961–1964, two firms in the sector were forced into bankruptcy. Several other firms in the sector have also been losing money; prices have been below their average costs, and they have been unable to arrange agreements raising prices to profitable levels. Further evidence of individual rather than industry-wide or trade-association price determination is seen in the reaction of companies to the inflation. When confronted with rises in the prices of their inputs, firms have not responded with identical sector-wide price adjustments. Rather, they have raised their prices individually, in varying percentages and with different timing, as individual managements have tried to make their own optimal adjustments. Finally, competition has also forced firms to make efforts at cutting their production costs. In recent years, almost all firms in the sector have used time-motion studies, conducted either by their own personnel or by consultants. Competitive pressures are the reason universally cited for these efforts.

Price competition is not mitigated by market imperfections which might be assumed important in a less-developed country. Personal friendship or similar national origin—for example, German supplier firms with German client firms—play little role in awarding contracts over lower bids from other companies. According to firms in the sector, at the most such connections may prompt companies to give an opportunity at "first refusal," that is, a chance to bid against a lower bid received from other sources. Moreover, although much of the sector's business is done with governmental or quasi-governmental agencies, even firms which have frequently lost on government tenders do not claim that differential political access determines contract awards.[2] Political connections are considered a simple cost item for institutional advertising and public relations expenditure, equally within the reach of all firms.[3]

In an effort to mitigate the pressures of price competition, firms have sought to differentiate their products. For example, firms have often entered new product lines in which they hoped to attain a degree of monopoly power. As was discussed in Chapter II, this has been an important theme in the sector's history. One firm pioneered in production of goods previously imported, and earned above-average profits, which soon attracted other firms who put pressure on margins. In recent years, when the range of domestic products has been too complete to permit easy product differentiation by this means, firms have competed actively on the basis of quality.

Higher-quality production is attained by use of better materials, superior production and control equipment, and manpower skills. Although there has usually been open competition in purchase of raw materials, market distortions may prevent equal access to the other inputs. Capital market imperfections may give differential access to the funds required for quality production and control equipment. Imperfect factor mobility and oligopsonistic

---

2. The absence of allegations of corruption in awarding of contract bids is all the more remarkable because in Brazil graft is perceived in almost all political transactions.

3. One imperfection that may exist in this market is related to the large "economic groups" with firms in different sectors of the economy. Some of the groups with operations in the chemical, metallurgical, and cement industries also have their own mechanical subsidiaries, from which they purchase most of their equipment. The "groups" follow this practice because they believe that their internal cost for such equipment is lower than prices of other suppliers. But because of the strong bias for autarky within these groups, they may not solicit outside bids even in cases where equipment could be supplied more cheaply by outside firms. The relative importance of these groups as potential customers, however, is much overshadowed by other clients.

skill markets such as we discussed in Chapter III may prevent skilled workers and staff from receiving their full marginal value product. Consequently, firms with these inputs can earn quasi-rents and higher returns from better-quality products. Because of these conditions, firms in the sector have placed a strong emphasis on achieving better-quality production. They have been especially sensitive to the possible gains of such an effort because of their competitive disadvantage in lower-quality products. As noted in Chapter II, smaller boiler shops, foundries, and machine shops with lower overhead costs have consistently underbid them in tenders for lower-quality products.

One aspect of this competition has been an effort to have minimum technical standards fixed by the government for certain types of equipment. An unspoken aim of this campaign has been the desire to reduce competitive pressure from the smaller firms, by fixing a lower boundary on the quality range available on industrial equipment. Firms have also concentrated on product lines with special quality requirements. For example, in recent years, firms in the sector have emphasized production of petrochemical and naval equipment. In the former case, contract tenders specified international, high-quality specifications. For naval equipment, international insurance has been available only for products meeting the quality requirements of *Lloyd's Register of Shipping.* Finally, within the sector, firms have also competed actively in terms of the quality/price range offered to clients.[4]

Credit terms have been another area of competition. Clients soliciting bids for equipment purchases give a prominent place to terms such as the amount of the initial payment, the scheduling of progress payments during production, and the conditions for finance after delivery. Credit terms have been especially important to clients because, as mentioned earlier, the domestic banking system has not played an important role in equipment financing.

4. In addition to objective product differentiation, some firms have also attempted to increase the inelasticity of their demand curves by artificial product differentiation. Through extensive institutional advertising, they have attempted to create a "name," a reputation for quality and dependability. This has been especially important in dealing with smaller potential client firms that do not have an internal technical staff and are unwilling to incur the information costs of differentiating among potential suppliers. Another reason for extensive institutional advertising is the effort to impress the government agencies that allocate investment funds and import licenses with the firms' technological competance and contribution to national industrial development.

Since sales are a product of both manufacturing and credit operations, the sector's firms have done much more in this respect. The availability of working capital to permit a firm to offer such credits has been an important competitive advantage.

Finally, with the acceleration of inflation, and the universal adoption within the sector of formal contracts adjusting delivery prices to cost rises from the date of the contract signing, firms have also competed with each other in the terms of their adjustment procedures. Individual companies have followed a wide variety of revaluation practices, for example, in costing adjustments for materials and for depreciation. Because some contracts have been more favorable to clients than others, they too have become an important aspect of competition.

REASONS FOR COMPETITION

EASE OF ENTRY

A basic factor conditioning the sector's market structure has been the excess capacity that developed after 1960. As mentioned earlier, this excess capacity appears to be a case of overbuilding that resulted from the way in which investment decisions in the sector were made. Although certain factors might have been considered serious barriers to entry, this did not prove to be the case, and excess capacity with its attendant pressures towards market rivalry could develop.

Capital requirements have not been a major restriction for participation in the sector.[5] As noted in Chapter II, the sector's capital requirements are both relatively low and without major indivisibilities. Access to the sector's specialized know-how has also been relatively open. Furthermore, although the previously established firms and the sector's trade association may have wanted to restrict entry, they were not able to obtain government sanction for such a policy. A similar absence of institutional barriers has also prevailed in other Brazilian industries, such as steel, cement, and paper, where existing firms also had a strong market position and excellent political access. Basic to the government's liberal attitude has been the feeling that with rapidly growing demand pressing upon domestic supply and foreign-

5. Use of the word "major" and other qualifiers throughout this paragraph refers to the fact that although neither capital requirements nor access to advanced technology were easily within the range of all Brazilian entrepreneurs, they were available to a sufficient number of companies to create overinvestment and excess capacity.

exchange resources, the country's economic development and its persistent balance-of-payments problem were best served by maximum expansion of local production capacity.

Because of the ease of entry, in the late 1950's and early 1960's firms were able to enter product lines which had formerly been dominated by one or two companies, thereby creating conditions for strong market rivalry. These pressures often became cumulative: new competition stimulated firms which had previously enjoyed monopolistic positions in some products to enter *other* markets where they had formerly not participated.

BARRIERS TO CARTELIZATION

Ease of entry and excess capacity were not, in themselves, enough to lead to a competitive market structure. Price fixing and cartelization could also result, were it not for certain difficulties which firms have had in reaching such arrangements.

First, efforts at price fixing have been hampered by the fact that different firms have different cost levels and cost structures, so that it has been difficult to agree on a common price. The firms' production equipment varies greatly in age and productivity. Thus labor and depreciation costs vary among companies, giving rise to different cost structures. Furthermore, some firms have much higher unit fixed costs than others, as a result of different overhead practices or greater excess capacity ratios. Because standard pricing procedures in the sector try to recover fixed costs, this has been an important barrier preventing establishment of common prices. Firms have also followed different practices in adjusting their costing and pricing to the effects of inflation. Procedures have been so heterogeneous that one trade association established courses for its firms' accountants to promote a degree of uniform practice. In the meantime, however, practices have varied so greatly among firms that, coupled with the differences in real cost structures, it has been difficult to establish agreements on price. Consequently, efforts at price fixing have soon disintegrated under the impact of the "discounts" offered by firms with lower costs.

There have also been serious problems in establishing agreement on a division of the market among various firms. The sector's history has been one of constant entry by new firms, domestic and foreign, and consequent instability in market shares. New firms entering the sector have usually gone through a period of intense competition with the established firms, in order to carve out part of the market. No sooner is some pattern of market shares reached than other entrants disturb the situation. The ease of "sideways entry" from other product markets, facilitated by nonspecificity of fabricating capacity, has also contributed to instability, for the number of participants in a given sub-sector depends on conditions in many other markets. The number of bidders on a petrochemical contract, for example, varies with conditions in the sugar-processing, shipbuilding, chemical, and railway equipment industries; for firms supplying those industries may divert their capacity to produce petrochemical equipment. In this situation, agreement on price fixing or market shares has been very difficult. In the words of one firm, "This is the Far West." Finally, there has been no firm with sufficient market power to enforce price leadership and market division upon the rest of the sector. Individual firms have adjusted to this situation of anarchy with diverse individual pricing and expansion strategies.

Such a situation of over-capacity and intense competition might appear well suited for a merger movement which would reduce the number of firms, retire excess capacity, and mitigate competitive pressures. In fact, however, no mergers have taken place. Apart from the problem of implicit market shares that would have to be decided in negotiating asset values, long-term expectations within the sector have worked against a merger movement. As noted in Chapter II, the firms believe that the Brazilian market for capital goods will grow rapidly in the future. Hence, neglecting the possibility of entry by new firms or considering themselves at a competitive advantage against potential entrants, they believe that their present capacity will be amply justified. Consequently, they have been reluctant to merge and leave the market, losing the— subjectively estimated—high profits of the future.

Institutional conditions have also militated against mergers. The owner-managers of the sector's family firms resist the reduction in their control of the firm and in their personal income (which is based on return to both capital and executive salaries) that mergers might entail.[6] The international firms have also been against

6. Whether their fears are justified is unimportant, since the very possibility has been enough to close the door to possible mergers.

consolidation. The other foreign firms whom they encounter in the sector are usually their arch rivals in home markets and third-country competition. For example, Mitsubuishi and Ishikawajima from Japan, Nordon and Creusot-Schneider of France, and Brown Boveri and General Electric all meet in the Brazilian sector's competition. For reasons of prestige, even if Brazilian market conditions warranted a merger, the home office would often veto any such "submission" to their rivals. Because of these conditions, although one foreign firm left the market by the expedient of closing its doors and sending home its expatriates, there has been no general merger movement retiring capacity and reducing competitive pressures within the sector.

Pressure on prices and quality has been enforced not only by competition among firms of the sector but also by the strong countervailing power of their clients. In their various product markets for chemical, petrochemical, metallurgical, paper-making, cement, and electrical equipment, firms of the sector usually confront oligopsonistic buyers with considerable bargaining power. These clients also have excellent political connections. The major purchasers of petrochemical, metallurgical, and electrical equipment are public-sector corporations with direct access to the President's Office. Major clients in the private sector, such as chemicals, paper, and cement, also have a strong political position. They are usually members of the large "economic groups," with appropriate connections, and can also make the politically strong claim of being industrialists in the "basic industries," promoting the country's economic development. Consequently, firms in the heavy-engineering sector are under strong pressure to make their bids as attractive as possible, for they must always consider the possibility that unless they are competitive in price and quality, particular equipment projects may be supplied from importation. Under these conditions, firms have attempted to attain international quality standards, and they have usually found it prudent to set prices as low as possible, that is, cost plus a minimum mark-up.

EFFECTS OF COMPETITION IN THE SECTOR

One result of the sector's market structure has been increased diversification in Brazilian capital goods supply. In the repeated efforts to escape competitive pressure by pioneering in new product lines, many new products have become available from domestic supply.

The sector's industrial organization has also had important effects on the factor market. With the pressures to produce better-quality products, demand has increased for the inputs necessary for improved technical standards: various types of equipment, skilled labor, technical personnel, and know-how. Not only has demand for these inputs grown, but inter-firm bidding in their purchase has increased too. As competition in the product market spilled over into the factor market, market power in the purchase of some inputs such as specific labor skills has been reduced.

Price competition has also put constant pressure on profits. Competing in contract bids against firms who are known to be losing money and anxious to cover even a part of their fixed costs, no firms have been able to set prices with unduly high margins. As a result, profits and prices in the sector are lower than they would be in a cartelized market. Competition has also enforced pressures for efficiency and cost cutting. As a result, firms have been receptive to the possibilities of increased efficiency through innovations in capital equipment, production engineering, and time-motion studies. Furthermore, increased efficiencies have been forcibly passed on, as external economies, to clients. This latter consideration is especially important because of the sector's strategic position as a supplier of goods for capital formation and economic growth. This leads us to our next subject, the economic effects of the sector's growth.

VIII

EFFECTS OF THE INDUSTRY'S GROWTH

INCOME CREATION AND ECONOMIC DIVERSIFICATION

In 1963, value added in the Brazilian capital goods industry amounted to over 1 billion dollars.[1] Starting from a base of some 306 million dollars, value added rose approximately 166 percent in real terms between 1949 and 1959, at an annual cumulative growth rate of 10.3 percent.[2] This can be compared with a 1949–1959 cumulative rate of 9.2 percent for Brazilian manufacturing as a whole, and 5.6 percent for aggregate real output.[3] Furthermore, most of the industry's inputs have been supplied from domestic sources; in 1949 its import-content was approximately 20 percent, and in 1959 about 12 percent.[4] Consequently, its rapidly expanding production qualified it as a "leading sector" stimulating the entire economy's growth.

1. IBRD, "Manufacturing Industry" ("Current Economic Position and Prospects of Brazil," vol. 5, mimeographed [Washington, D.C., February 1965]), Appendix A. The same source estimated gross output in the capital goods industry at 2,329 million dollars in 1963.

2. The figure is based on data in IBGE, *Censo Industrial* (Rio de Janeiro, 1963). For the estimation procedures followed, see Chap. II, n. 20, above. In heavy-engineering products, output in 1964 amounted to approximately 210 million dollars, of which some 141 million dollars were value added. This figure is from ECLA, "Brasil: La Exportación de Manufacturas, sus Antecedéntes y sus Possibilidades," mimeographed (Santiago, Chile, 1966), p. 26.

3. Data from the *Censo Industrial* enable us to discuss the consequences of this income creation for one particular factor of production, labor. In 1959, there were approximately 238,000 workers in the capital goods industry, and, as the accompanying table indicates, their wages were considerably higher, 37% in 1959, than the manufacturing industry average.

Average Wages Per Worker in the Mechanical Industry and in Other Brazilian Industries (Indices)

Industry	1949	1959
Mechanical	100	100
Textile	61	69
Metallurgical	89	97
Paper	68	83
Chemical	70	93
Manufacturing-industry average	71	73

4. For the data sources used in these estimates, see n. 9 below.

Table VIII-1. Percentage of Value Added by Industries in the Manufacturing Sector

Sector	1949	1959	1963
Consumer Goods	52.5	38.7	34.6
Intermediate Products	25.1	28.0	30.8
Capital Goods	22.4	33.3	34.6
	100.0	100.0	100.0

Source: IBRD, "Manufacturing Industry" ("Current Economic Position and Prospects of Brazil," vol. 5, mimeographed [Washington, D.C., February 1965]), p. 1.

The industry's growth has also contributed to the diversification of the Brazilian economy. Table VIII–1 indicates its increasing importance within Brazilian manufacturing. The capital goods industry has come to produce more than a third of value added in the manufacturing sector, while the share of consumer goods production has declined sharply. Table VIII–2 presents comparative data on the relative importance of capital goods production

Table VIII-2. Percentage Share of the Electrical and Mechanical Industries in the Industrial Sectors of Ten Countries

Country	Total industrial employment	Total industrial value added
Austria, 1955	10.0	n.a.
Belgium, 1955	10.0	n.a.
France, 1955	11.0	n.a.
Greece, 1955	3.0	n.a.
Italy, 1955	11.0	n.a.
United Kingdom, 1955	20.0	19.0
United States, 1955	18.0	17.0
West Germany, 1955	17.0	17.0
Peru, 1959	0.9	0.3
Brazil, 1959	6.0	7.0

n.a. = data not available.
Sources: For Brazil, computed from data in *Censo Industrial;* for the other countries, ECE, "Production and Export of Capital Goods in the Fields of Mechanical and Electrical Engineering," mimeographed (E/ECE/439, 1962), p. 2.

(defined somewhat more narrowly by the ECE) and indicates the extent to which Brazilian industrial structure has come to resemble that of the advanced countries.[5]

REDUCED DEPENDENCE ON IMPORTS FOR CAPITAL FORMATION

Development of domestic capital goods production has also reduced Brazil's dependence upon external sources of investment goods supply. This has attracted considerable interest for several reasons.

First, many Brazilians believe that an economy whose capital goods supply is independent of outside forces can be more autonomous in determining its rate of capital formation and growth. Apart from their interest in economic independence pure and simple, they assume that this will be accompanied by greater political and cultural autonomy. Domestic capital goods production has also aroused interest because of immediate policy considerations. Brazilian economic administrators and politicians must always remember the country's experience during World War I, the Great Depression, and World War II, when difficulties in importing producers' goods adversely affected investment and economic growth. Greater domestic capital goods supply could not have avoided all of the economic difficulties engendered by those international events; but it could have mitigated their retarding effects on domestic capital formation.

In more recent years, the question is posed in the context of Brazil's chronic balance-of-payments problem. Assuming, as most Brazilian economists do: (1) that the prospects are poor for expanding exports *pari passu* with an acceptable rate of growth because of international demand conditions; and (2) that possibilities for further import substitution are limited by increasing inelasticity of substitution with respect to relative prices, as between domestic production and imports for the other products (like crude petroleum) remaining on the import list, then comparative advantage would make it cheaper to acquire investment goods through domestic production than through foreign trade.[6] Further

---

5. The definition of the Economic Commission for Europe excludes output of the transportation-equipment and the metallurgical industries, which in Brazil turn out relatively large quantities of producers' goods.

6. As suggested below, this approach may not in fact be valid.

assuming price-elastic demand for capital goods, then *ceteris paribus*, the rate of capital formation depends on the degree to which domestic production replaces imports in supply of capital goods. As mentioned in Chapter I, much of the Brazilian and Latin American policy interest in development of capital goods and other "heavy industries" derives from just such considerations: the prospect of freeing domestic investment and growth from the constraints of foreign-exchange supply.

Development of domestic investment goods production has indeed greatly reduced dependence on imports for investment goods, both in equipment supply and in total fixed-capital formation. As noted in Chapter VI, in value terms the domestic industry supplied approximately 61 percent of all Brazilian equipment purchases in 1947–1949, and 72 percent in 1957–1959.[7] These current-value figures actually understate the magnitude of the shift to domestic supply; for, as we have seen, during these years the cruzeiro price of imports increased more rapidly than the

TABLE VIII-3. Ratio of the Quantum of Equipment supplied from Imports to the Quantum Supplied Domestically (Index: 1947–1949 = 100)

Year	$\frac{Q_m}{Q_n}$	Year	$\frac{Q_m}{Q_n}$
1947	124	1954	59
1948	95	1955	44
1949	81	1956	33
1950	86	1957	38
1951	116	1958	65
1952	114	1959	61
1953	66		

Sources: For the quantum series on imports, data from "Auge y Declinación del Proceso de Sustitución de Importaciones en el Brasil," *Boletín Económico de América Latina*, 9 (March 1964), Table 7-A, adjusted by the Machinery Prices Deflator of the Bureau of Labor Statistics, were used. For the quantum series on domestic supply, current value figures were deflated by the index of metallurgical prices. From these two series an index of relative quantum supply of capital goods was calculated, and this in turn was recomputed to a 1947–1949 = 100 base.

7. See Table VI-1, above.

TABLE VIII-4. Domestic Supply as a Percentage of Total Supply of Cement and Metallurgical Products

Product	1949	1958
Cement	75	100
Metallurgical Products	78	88

Source: "Auge y Declinación del Proceso de Sustitución de Importaciones en el Brasil," *Boletín Económico de América Latina,* 9 (March 1964), Tables 25 and 31.

cruzeiro price of domestic products, because of the depreciation of the real exchange rate. To correct for this movement of relative prices, Table VIII–3 sets out quantum data on domestic and imported equipment supply.

The quantum data show an even greater shift, of approximately 45 percent, toward domestic supply between 1947–1949 and 1957–1959.[8] Furthermore, as seen in Table VIII–4, import substitution also occurred in the other investment goods industries,

8. Of course, the increasing relative importance of domestic capital goods supply might be due to another factor—an absolute decline in imports. This would not indicate greater "independence" but a reduction in imports and perhaps of aggregate capital formation. To check this possibility, we present the figures on the quantum trend alongside data on annual equipment imports.

Imports and Ratio of the Quantum of Domestic and Imported Equipment, Brazil 1947–1959

Year	Q_m/Q_n Index: 1947–1959 = 100	Imports of Equipment (millions of dollars)
1947	124	424
1948	95	388
1949	81	350
1950	86	409
1951	116	637
1952	114	672
1953	66	298
1954	59	371
1955	44	268
1956	33	220
1957	38	332
1958	65	335
1959	61	380

In 1953 and in 1956, the increase in "independence" shown in the quantum index does reflect declines in the absolute value of imports. For the other years and for the period as a whole, however, the evolution of the quantum index indicates that even with imports maintained, domestic supply became a more important source of equipment supply than it was in the beginning of the period.

cement and metallurgy. As a result of these developments, the import content of Brazilian fixed-capital formation declined from approximately 31 percent in 1949 to about 22 percent in 1959.[9] As Table VIII–5 indicates, this has given Brazilian fixed investment a relatively low import content compared with other Latin American countries.

TABLE VIII-5. Import Content of Fixed-Capital Formation in Eight Latin American Countries

Country	Percent	Country	Percent
Bolivia, 1955–1959	65	Venezuela, 1955–1961	34
Chile, 1955–1961	59	Colombia, 1959–1961	31
Peru, 1959–1961	46	Mexico, 1955–1961	30
Ecuador, 1959–1961	41	Brazil, 1959	22

Sources: Data for the countries other than Brazil were computed from material in *The Economic Development of Latin America in the Post-War Period* (New York: United Nations, 1964), pp. 91, 98, 117. The import coefficient for the countries (e.g., Mexico and Colombia) with a domestic equipment industry is understated, because the figures do not include estimates of the import content of domestically produced equipment.

EFFECTS OF DECREASED DEPENDENCE ON IMPORTED CAPITAL GOODS

Increased domestic supply of capital goods has meant a higher elasticity of aggregate supply with respect to domestic money

9. The following tabulation presents estimates of the import content of the various components of fixed investment, as percentages of total fixed-capital formation.

	1949	1959
Construction	3%	0%
Imported Equipment	20%	16%
Domestic Equipment	8%	6%
	31%	22%

This Table is calculated from FGV data on the distribution of fixed investment. Data on domestic and imported cement supply are from Table 31, "Auge y Declinación del Proceso de Sustitución de Importaciones en el Brasil," *Boletín Económico de América Latina*, 9 (March 1964). The import-content of domestic equipment was calculated with the aid of data from the *Censo Industrial* and a 1960 survey by the members of the São Paulo Association of Equipment Manufacturers, kindly made available by Dr. Einar Kok. Figures for ferrous and nonferrous metal supply are from América Barbosa de Oliveira, "Mercado Presente e Futuro do Aço," *A Boletim da Associação Brasileira de Metais*, 16 (January 1963), Appendix Tables 1 and 4; and "Auge y Declinación," p. 47 and Appendix Tables 1 and 4. These data indicate an approximate import content for domestically produced equipment of 20% and 12% for 1949 and 1959, respectively.

income. This is especially important in the context of a less-developed economy. Under conditions of export stagnation, limited economic diversification and income-inelastic domestic supply have been cited as major structural reasons for inflation.[10] With this development in Brazil, however, increases in internal demand without concomitant increases in imports will generate higher real output rather than inflationary price rises.[11]

The declining import content of fixed-capital formation has also meant a higher domestic investment multiplier. As leakages of investment expenditure into imports declined, the large increases in the volume of investment during this period had an increasing multiplier effect on national income. In the relatively high value of its investment multiplier Brazil is significantly different from most other less-developed economies.[12] Moreover, because domestic supply has kept pace and, indeed, through import substitution has exceeded the growth in investment expenditure, investment has become an increasingly important determinant of national income. Here, too, Brazil differs from many underdeveloped economies, in which exportation rather than investment is the major determinant of GNP.[13] With some 78 percent of all investment goods supplied domestically and fixed capital formation averaging 16 percent of GNP, domestic investment goods supply constitutes about 13 percent of GNP. This contrasts with an export sector of approximately 8 percent of GNP. Under these conditions, the Brazilian

10. For a good example of this viewpoint, see Oswaldo Sunkel, "El Francaso de las Políticas de Establización en el Contexto del Proceso de Desarrollo Latinoaméricano," *El Trimestre Económico*, 30, no. 4 (September 1963), 627–29. Cf. V. K. R. V. Rao, "Investment, Income, and the Multiplier in an Underdeveloped Economy," *Indian Economic Review* (February 1952), reprinted in *The Economics of Underdevelopment*, ed. A. N. Agarwala and S. P. Singh (New York, 1963), esp. pp. 209–212.

11. Gordon Smith has pointed out to me that if the conditions making for "structuralist" inflation diminished, those making for "monetarist" inflation increased in Brazil during these years. The government's budget deficit rose sharply, from 0.3% of GNP in 1947–1949 to 4.7% in 1961–1963. Avoiding such a dichotomized interpretation of the Brazilian inflation we might say that if the constraint on the annual rate of inflation has been a maximum tolerable rate of inflation or its acceleration, increased elasticity of aggregate supply has permitted larger budget deficits than would otherwise have been feasible.

12. Dudley Seers has even argued that Keynesian models of income determination and growth are largely irrelevant in the context of underdeveloped countries because of the very different values of the domestic investment multiplier, due to great leakages of investment expenditure into imports. See his article, "The Limitations of the Special Case," *Bulletin of the Oxford Institute of Economics and Statistics*, 24 (May 1962).

13. Cf., e.g., H. C. Wallich, *Monetary Problems of an Export Economy* (Cambridge, Mass., 1951), pp. 125–27; and J. V. Levin, *The Export Economies* (Cambridge, Mass., 1962), *passim*.

economy is more autonomous in determining its level of aggregate income than many other less-developed economies. This can, of course, work in both directions, and the Brazilian economy is now far more capable than previously of generating its own business cycle. For example, the slackening of economic growth after 1962 was probably aggravated by a downward multiplier effect of reduced investment throughout the economy.

EFFECTS ON CAPITAL FORMATION

As mentioned earlier, much of the enthusiasm and policy interest in Brazil concerning this industry derives from the assumption that increased domestic capital goods supply is synonymous with lifting a severe constraint on capital formation imposed by income-inelastic import supply. Any a priori conclusions and optimism in this regard, however, are brought up very sharply by the experience of postwar Argentina. A study by Hayn has shown that the relative price of capital goods in Argentina has increased by approximately 50 percent since the 1930's.[14] This movement of relative prices was so great as to wipe out a 50-percent rise in the gross investment coefficient, calculated in current prices. Although investment rose from a prewar figure of 13 percent to 18–22 percent of GNP, in real terms there had been no increase at all. One implication of the study was that import substitution in capital goods may have been partly responsible for the relative price movement. Later work disaggregating the Argentine capital goods price index demonstrated that, on the contrary, the main culprits in the relative price rise were imported equipment and construction.[15] Nevertheless, the moral of the story remains, suggesting caution in evaluating the effects of import substitution in capital goods on capital formation.

The Argentine experience points to two possible pernicious consequences. First, if increased domestic supply entails a rise in the relative price of capital goods, investment may be reduced as the cost of capital assets rises relative to the future income streams they will produce. Secondly, there is the possibility that government protectionism fostering import substitution in capital goods might

14. R. Hayn, "Capital Formation and Argentina's Price-Cost Structure, 1935–58," *Review of Economics and Statistics*, 44 (August 1962).

15. Carlos F. Diaz-Alejandro, "Relative Prices and Capital Formation in Argentina," mimeographed (Yale University, Economic Growth Center, 1965), Table 1.

raise their cost above world market levels. This increase in costs would again reduce investment and growth, compared to what they would be if the cheaper imports were available.[16] Consequently, any treatment of the effects of the domestic capital goods industry's growth on capital formation must focus on prices: on movements in the relative price of capital goods, and domestic prices as compared with imports.

Within this perspective—which is confined to considerations of absolute advantage—the Brazilian experience appears to have been favorable. Although a price index of domestically produced equipment is not available, it seems clear that there was no pernicious movement of relative prices. As noted in Chapter VI, through 1962, the domestic capital goods industry was under the full pressure of price competition from imports, which were generally available with preferential exchange rates and without tariff duties. The equipment industry was the only industry producing internationally traded goods which was open to such world market price competition. Therefore, it seems unlikely that equipment prices rose relative to the prices of other industries, which had large increases in protection during the postwar period.[17]

Furthermore, as regards comparison of Brazilian equipment prices with world market prices, the situation also appears generally favorable. As noted, the domestic equipment industry was able to expand very rapidly despite active price competition with imports. ECLA study groups have also made direct price comparisons for two important equipment sectors, heavy-engineering products and machine tools, and found them generally competitive at world market levels.[18] These comparisons, moreover, understate the

16. Diaz-Alejandro, "Relative Prices," sec. II, p. 3, suggests that despite the sharp movement in relative prices, profits were high enough to justify investment and, indeed, that the demand for capital goods in Argentina was so inelastic with respect to price that real capital formation was not retarded, because savings increased enough to compensate for the additional cost of investment goods. Without the movement of relative prices, however, the same volume of savings could have financed even higher rates of real investment and growth, or similar rates of capital formation could have been achieved at a lower welfare cost.

17. In addition to other import restrictions which were raised continually through the postwar period, tariffs were also increased, reaching a range of 30–80% ad valorem. See Santiago Macario, "Proteccionismo e Industrialización en América Latina," *Boletín Económico de América Latina*, 9 (March 1964), 75.

18. ECLA, *Basic Equipment in Brazil* (*The Manufacture of Industrial Machinery and Equipment in Latin America*, vol. 1 [New York: United Nations, 1963]), pp. 59–62; *Las Máquinas-Herramientas en el Brasil* (*La Fabricación de Maquinarias y Equipos Industriales en América Latina*, vol. 2 [New York: United Nations, 1962]), p. 40.

contribution of the domestic capital goods industry to capital formation, for they are made on the basis of average prices and the average exchange rate. When considered in relation to *marginal* import supply, the contribution of the domestic capital goods industry to Brazilian capital formation appears considerably greater, particularly since the last half of the 1950's.

As Table VIII–6 shows, in contrast to earlier years, after 1955 Brazilian imports did not grow as rapidly as GNP. Between 1955 and 1961, national income rose 52 percent, as compared with a 6-percent increase in the supply of imports. Viewed in this perspective, import substitution appears even more strongly as an economic source of capital goods supply.

This is, however, only a partial analysis. The real question is whether the export stagnation which lay behind this income-inelastic supply of imports was necessary. There is some evidence that it was not; but that it was caused rather by ill-conceived

TABLE VIII-6. GNP and Imports in Brazil, 1948–1964

Year	GNP	Imports
	(Indices: 1954 = 100)	
1948	73	44
1949	77	51
1950	81	63
1951	85	95
1952	90	92
1953	93	70
1954	100	100
1955	107	89
1956	109	84
1957	116	104
1958	124	102
1959	133	113
1960	142	114
1961	152	106
1962	161	99
1963	164	99
1964	169	84

Sources: Data on GNP are from FGV. Data on imports are from index 117 in *Conjuntura Económica.*

Brazilian policies which discouraged exports of products other than coffee.[19] Had more effective policies toward exportation been adopted, the economy might well have enjoyed a more adequate flow of imports. Hence relative prices would not have moved to favor local producers for some new equipment products, which could have been acquired more economically through foreign trade than through import substitution.[20] Within the constraints of the export policies that were actually adopted, however, the expansion of domestic capital goods production did enable Brazil to avoid the worst of both worlds—stagnant foreign trade *and* stagnant domestic supply of the goods needed for capital formation.

19. See Nathaniel H. Leff, "Export Stagnation and Autarkic Development in Brazil," *Quarterly Journal of Economics*, 81 (May 1967), 286–301, and chap. 5 of Nathaniel H. Leff, *Economic Policy-Making and Development in Brazil* (New York, 1968).

20. For a similar case in which evaluations at the sectoral level depend heavily on macroeconomic analysis and ultimately on interpretation of the country's foreign trade conditions, see William A. Johnson, *The Steel Industry of India* (Cambridge, Mass., 1966), pp. 37, 115–122. These experiences support Hollis Chenery's stress on the need for planning techniques that determine a country's optimal pattern of trade simultaneously with its optimal investment allocations. See his "Comparative Advantage and Development Policy," in The American Economic Association and the Royal Economic Society, *Surveys of Economic Theory*, 2 (New York, 1966), 145.

IX

THE CAPITAL GOODS INDUSTRY AND FUTURE BRAZILIAN DEVELOPMENT

Capital goods production developed relatively early in Brazilian industrialization, and by 1947–1949 the domestic industry supplied approximately 61 percent of all Brazilian producers' equipment. In the 1950's the industry expanded especially rapidly, growing at a rate higher than that of Brazilian manufacturing as a whole and increasing its share to 75 percent of the total market for equipment. This growth was achieved, moreover, without import restrictions and, indeed, in active price competition with imports which, as part of the government's general development policy, were made available to investors at a preferential exchange rate. The industry's experience offers a contrast with what might be called the "black legend" of Brazilian industrialization: namely, that all Brazilian industry is high-cost as compared with world market prices and that import substitution is achieved only by means of substantial government protection.[1]

As we saw in Chapters II–IV, the supply of factors for capital goods production has been relatively elastic. Capital was attracted to such an extent that considerable excess capacity existed in the industry even before the slackening of aggregate Brazilian growth in 1963. The supply of technically educated personnel and skilled manpower has likewise increased rapidly in response to demand conditions. Firms have also been able easily to enter new product lines involving "complex technology," either on the basis of their own technical competence or through licensing agreements with companies in the advanced countries. Factor supply has in addition been income-elastic: through profit reinvestment and learning in the course of production, output in one period generated the capital, trained personnel, and "know-how" for production in subsequent periods. There is no reason to expect that the supply of inputs will be less elastic in the future. Consequently, the industry's growth should be largely a function of its demand conditions.

1. I borrow the phrase "black legend," in the context of Latin American industrialization, from Hugh Schwartz.

177

Because, as mentioned earlier, export sales have been limited by imperfections in the international equipment market, the industry's demand depends mainly on the domestic market. As we saw in Chapter V, this has increased proportionately with the growth of real income, apparently constrained by the supply of savings to finance capital formation. Real savings, in turn, have increased *pari passu* with national income. Unit income-elasticity of savings has persisted despite economic conditions and policy measures which might have been expected to raise marginal savings rates.

For some time, an increase in the domestic industry's market share enabled it to grow more rapidly than aggregate demand for capital goods. The possibilities for further import substitution now appear limited, however, because imports consist largely of products which have special supply characteristics or which are tied to foreign credits. As suggested in Chapter VI, if long-term Brazilian growth resumes in the previous pattern, with pressure on the real exchange rate, investors may well prefer domestic credits to finance their equipment purchases; and this may permit some further expansion of the industry's market share. Otherwise, unless marginal savings rates rise to increase the aggregate savings coefficient, the industry's demand and output should grow in proportion with aggregate Brazilian income.

These conclusions do not suggest that the capital goods industry can fill the role of "leading sector," for which it has been proposed, in future Brazilian growth.[2] The industry has already passed through the phase when because of an increase in its share of the market, its output could grow more rapidly than aggregate domestic demand for capital goods. Consequently, the capital goods industry seems to have joined the list of "vegetative" industries, which, after a period of import substitution, grow proportionately with national income.[3] Hence, Brazilian policy-makers may be well advised to look elsewhere for a stimulus to rapid economic growth in future years.

2. This suggestion was often heard among Brazilian economic policymakers in the early 1960's. See the discussion in "Auge y Declinación del Proceso de Sustitución de Importaciones in el Brasil," *Boletín Económico de América Latina*, 9 (March, 1964), 59–62.

3. In ECLA studies, "vegetative" is used to describe industries such as textiles in which import substitution has already given the domestic industry the great part of the internal market, so that on the assumption of unit income-elasticity and no price elasticity effects, demand and output are expected to grow only in accordance with the growth of GNP.

Our discussion also indicates caution concerning the suggestion ⌈that development of domestic capital goods supply will lead to accelerated rates of capital formation and growth.⌋ As noted earlier, the general view in Brazil has been that investment and growth were constrained by income-inelastic supply of investment goods, as a result of extreme dependence on (inelastic) supply of imports for most investment needs.[4] This implies a model which may be relevant for some less-developed countries: *ex ante* savings and investment exceed the capacity to import investment goods, and capital formation is retarded. In such a case, domestic capital goods production would make it possible to supply this repressed demand, and promote higher rates of capital formation. In the words of one observer, development of the domestic capital goods industry means "the definitive conquering of the barrier which the capacity to import imposed on capital formation."[5]

As noted earlier, import substitution may have prevented a rise in the relative price of investment goods, and enabled the economy to maintain a constant real rate of capital formation without a rising savings ratio. Import substitution in capital goods—which, as we have seen, had proceeded very far by the middle 1950's—did not, however, lead to higher rates of capital formation. Moreover, our previous discussion indicates that this model of capital formation constrained by import supply may be largely irrelevant to Brazil. As noted in Chapter VIII, in the postwar years through 1954, imports expanded more rapidly than the (high) rates of aggregate growth. By the time import constraints did apply, after 1955, domestic production of equipment—and *a fortiori* of construction materials—had proceeded so far that imports supplied only a small percentage of all investment goods.

Furthermore, many of these imports have been maintained not because of conditions on the supply side; indeed, the equipment imported has often been in product lines where domestic firms had excess capacity. Rather, as we have seen, imports have been maintained largely because of demand conditions—reliance on foreign savings, either in the form of supplier credits or of direct foreign investment, which have been tied to equipment imports.

---

4. Cf., for example, the citations from Celso Furtado in Chap. I and his *Development and Underdevelopment*, trans. R. W. de Aguiar and E. C. Drysdale (Berkeley, 1964), pp. 150–51.

5. Celso Furtado, *Desenvolvimento e Subdesenvolvimento*, 2 ed. (Rio de Janeiro, 1963), p. 242.

This suggests a situation in which *ex ante* investment is greater than domestic savings, and, when possible, part of the difference is made up from foreign savings. Putting aside the question of whether recent rates of Brazilian capital formation have been in some sense sub-optimal, the constraint on raising them has been posed by domestic savings, and not by the capacity to import investment goods.

Finally, although import substitution has greatly reduced the Brazilian economy's dependence on imports of capital goods, this does not mean that its growth possibilities are now independent of foreign trade conditions.[6] Although capital goods (and consumer products) are now available mainly from domestic supply, and the economy's aggregate import coefficient is relatively low (8 percent), many key raw material and intermediate products are still supplied from importation. There is, in fact, some evidence that the slackening of aggregate growth in 1963 was initiated by income-inelastic supply of these inputs.[7] Thus, quite apart from the considerations of comparative advantage which were cited at the end of Chapter VIII, import substitution in capital goods has not freed Brazil from possible import constraints, and Brazilian planners cannot neglect the place of exports in future growth.

6. The following quotation from the 1962 Brazilian development plan indicates the optimism that some Brazilian planners felt in this regard: "On reaching a phase of development where the process of capital formation leans mainly on our own production of equipment, the development of the Brazilian economy has come to depend on its own internal dynamics. Thus, no matter how important the external factors still may be, the rate of growth is determined mainly by . . . domestic market conditions . . . A lag in the external demand does not anymore, necessarily, result in a general slump in economic activity . . ." See *Three-Year Plan for Economic and Social Development* [*Plano Trienal*] (Rio de Janeiro, December 1962), pp. 18, 25–26.

7. See Nathaniel H. Leff, "Import Constraints and Development: Causes of the Recent Decline of Brazilian Economic Growth," *Review of Economics and Statistics*, 49 (November 1967).

INDEX

Agricultural tools industry, concentration ratio, 106n
Agriculture: growth, *1947–1961*, 1; as client for heavy-engineering products, 9; share in equipment purchases, 103
Algeria, savings rates and foreign investments, 119n
Anuario Estatístico, 69n
Argentina, 8, 35n; immigration to, 53n; percentage of equipment expenditure supplied by imports, 133; domestic supply of equipment, 134; price increase for capital goods, 173, 174n
Army, Brazilian, 9, 10
Associação Brasileira de Metais, 64
Australia, immigration policy, 53n
Automobile industry, 37; concentration, 106n; tariff exemption, 140
Automotive equipment industry, 6, 7, 20n; engineer inputs, 85n; effect on quality of capital goods production, 143–144
Azevedo, Fernando de, 59n

Baer, quoted, 13n
Banco do Brasil, 106, 118
Banco do Estado de São Paulo, 29n
Banks, banking, 7, 21, 29n, 106, 118, 151, 152; functions performed by local producers, 15–16
Barão de Mauá, 19n
Becker, Gary, 66n, 71n
Boiler products industry, 21, 22, 37; diversification in, 24; meets international standards, 142
Boiler shops, competitive advantages of, 160
Brasília, 104n
Brazil, government of: role in growth of heavy-engineering products sector, 22, 37–38; welcomes foreign investments, 25–26; decision on foreign suppliers credits, 34n; and "bunching" of foreign investments, 35; curtails royalty payments, 89; effect on equipment market, 104; and elastic supply of cheap capital, 106; efforts to promote domestic savings, investment, 117–118

Brazilian National Development Bank, 122n; position on financing domestic capital goods purchases, 150, 155
Brown Boveri, 164

Capital: original sources for domestic firms, 16; outside, for heavy-engineering sector, 20–21; formation, and expanded participation of public sector, 104; formation, and reduced dependence on imports for, 168–176; formation, and barrier of import capacity, 179; cheap, elastic supply of, 106; and excess capacity, 177
Capital goods industry: implications of growth, 2–4, 166–176, 177; defined, 4; growth, *1929–1945*, 11–15; demand, 102–131 (*see also* Demand); division of the market, 132–156 (*see also* Domestic production; Imports); income creation and economic diversification, 166–168; reduced dependence on imports for capital formation, 168–176; and future Brazilian development, 177–180
Carneiro, 119n
Cartelization, barriers to, 162–164
Cement industry, 5, 8; tariff exemption, 140; mechanical subsidiaries, 159n; absence of institutional barriers, 161; and political position of clients, 164; shift toward domestic supply, 170, 171
Cement-making equipment industry, 92n
Censo Industrial, 166n
Chemical industry, 5, 32, 85n, 103, 163; percentage of skilled workers in, 43; engineers as percentage of total work force, 45; engineer inputs, 85n; concentration, 106n; savings rates and foreign investments, 119n; tariff exemption, 140; import coefficient, 148; mechanical subsidiaries, 159n; and oligopsonistic buyers, 164; average wages per worker, 166n
Chenery, Hollis B., 119n, 176n
Coffee industry, 9, 10; sales in early postwar period, 112; effect of Korean War on, 133n; price inelasticity of demand, 135; and export trade, 176

A

Withdrawn

BISHOP'S UNIVERSITY
LIBRARY
LENNOXVILLE